DAUGHTERS
OF THE DUST

DAUGHTERS OF THE DUST

*The Making of an
African American Woman's
Film*

BY JULIE DASH

THE NEW PRESS · 1992 · NEW YORK CITY

PUBLISHED IN THE UNITED STATES BY THE NEW PRESS, NEW YORK.
DISTRIBUTED BY W.W. NORTON & COMPANY, INC.

Dash, Julie.
Daughters of the dust: the making of an African American woman's film/by Julie Dash with Toni Cade Bambara and Bell Hooks.
p. cm.
Includes the screenplay for the film, Daughters of the dust.   Includes bibliographical references.
ISBN 1-56584-029-1 (cloth)   ISBN 1-56584-030-5 (pbk.)

1. Daughters of the dust (Motion picture) 2. Afro-Americans in motion pictures. 3. Dash, Julie. 4. Afro-American motion picture producers and directors. I. Bambara, Toni Cade. II. Hooks, Bell. III. Daughters of the dust (motion picture) IV. Title.
PN1997.D313343D3 1991
791.43'72—dc20
92-50333
CIP

PRINTED IN THE UNITED STATES

9 8 7 6 5 4 3

GRATEFUL ACKNOWLEDGMENT IS MADE TO THE FOLLOWING FOR
PERMISSION TO USE PREVIOUSLY PUBLISHED MATERIAL:
"IBO LANDING" PASSAGES FROM *Praisesong for the Widow* BY PAULE MARSHALL.
REPRINTED BY PERMISSION OF THE PUTNAM PUBLISHING GROUP © 1983.
"THUNDER, PERFECT MIND," FROM THE NAG HAMMADI LIBRARY,
EDITED BY JAMES M. ROBINSON © 1978 BY E. J. BRILL.
REPRINTED BY PERMISSION OF HARPERCOLLINS PUBLISHERS.

ESTABLISHED IN 1990 AS A MAJOR ALTERNATIVE TO THE LARGE, COMMERCIAL PUBLISHING
HOUSES, THE NEW PRESS IS INTENDED TO BE THE FIRST FULL-SCALE NONPROFIT AMERICAN
BOOK PUBLISHER OUTSIDE OF THE UNIVERSITY PRESSES. THE PRESS IS OPERATED EDITORIALLY
IN THE PUBLIC INTEREST, RATHER THAN FOR PRIVATE GAIN; IT IS COMMITTED TO PUBLISHING
IN INNOVATIVE WAYS WORKS OF EDUCATIONAL, CULTURAL, AND COMMUNITY VALUE, WHICH
DESPITE THEIR INTELLECTUAL MERITS MIGHT NOT NORMALLY BE "COMMERCIALLY VIABLE."

A videocassette of Daughters of the Dust *can be ordered from Kino International by calling 1-800-562-3330*

*for my mother, Rhudine, and
my daughter, N'zinga.*

*Every woman extends backward into her mother
and forward to her daughter.*

— C. G. JUNG

Acknowledgments

I want to express my gratitude to the following people:

My family for loving me unconditionally and always believing in me. With special thanks to my mother, for putting me in a gypsy cab three nights a week to attend a film production workshop in the Studio Museum in Harlem in 1968.

To filmmaker Neema Barnette, my confidante, who has the courage to speak the truth regardless of the outcome.

Michelle Materre, Katheryn Bowser, Marlin L. Adams, and Mark Walton of the KJM 3 Entertainment group, and "Brother Kojo."

Sam Mattingley, my publicist.

Ben Hill, Monica Dotten, my manager and his assistant, and my attorneys, Stephen Barnes and Maria Perez.

Dr. Margaret Washington Creel, my historical adviser, who unselfishly took me under her protective wing.

Amy Carey, my film editor and friend for being there throughout, and afterward.

John Barnes, for his spiritual wisdom and guidance, which continues on long after he completed the original musical score of *Daughters*.

Tommy Burns, Keith Ward, Terry Bailey, and Sonja Avery for just being there for me.

Karma Bambara, my assistant, for her consistent good work and wonderful presence.

Michael Simanga, for showing up in my life just at the right time as a business partner and friend.

A.J., my coproducer and cinematographer, for sharing my vision and helping my dream come true.

And the editors at The New Press, David Sternbach and Dawn Davis, for making this book a reality.

Table of Contents

AUNT GERTIE'S RED RICE

1 CUP OF SOUTH CAROLINA WHITE RICE (DO NOT USE CONVERTED RICE)

2 CUPS OF WATER

1 CLOVE OF GARLIC

½ CUP OF CHOPPED ONIONS

½ CUP OF CHOPPED BELL PEPPERS

1 CAN OF TOMATO SAUCE

5 STRIPS OF BACON (OR SMOKED TURKEY)

Place the rice in a large bowl of water and scrub the rice between your hands. Keep changing the water until it is clear of starch. Pour off the water.

Use a deep, heavy pot with a lid. Cook the bacon or, if you prefer, smoked turkey with ¼ cup of vegetable oil in the bottom of the pot. Add your onions, peppers, garlic and cook until they are done. Add the tomato sauce and 2 cups of water. When the sauce begins to boil, add the rice. Use a fork to make sure the rice is evenly distributed in the tomato sauce. Never stir the rice once it begins to boil. "Never put a spoon in rice that's cooking…" When the rice begins to boil, lower the heat. Wrap a wet brown paper bag around the lid of the pot and cover. Slow-cook. "Every grain must stand on its own. Every grain must be red." Slow-cook until the rice absorbs all of the sauce.

Red rice tastes even better the next day.

MOMMY DASH'S GUMBO*

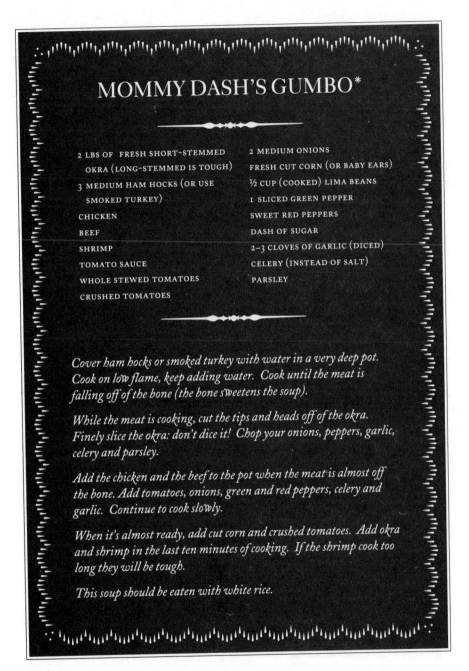

2 LBS OF FRESH SHORT-STEMMED OKRA (LONG-STEMMED IS TOUGH)

3 MEDIUM HAM HOCKS (OR USE SMOKED TURKEY)

CHICKEN

BEEF

SHRIMP

TOMATO SAUCE

WHOLE STEWED TOMATOES

CRUSHED TOMATOES

2 MEDIUM ONIONS

FRESH CUT CORN (OR BABY EARS)

½ CUP (COOKED) LIMA BEANS

1 SLICED GREEN PEPPER

SWEET RED PEPPERS

DASH OF SUGAR

2–3 CLOVES OF GARLIC (DICED)

CELERY (INSTEAD OF SALT)

PARSLEY

As with many gourmets, Mommy Dash doesn't use precise measurements. For best results, rely on your own sense of taste.

Cover ham hocks or smoked turkey with water in a very deep pot. Cook on low flame, keep adding water. Cook until the meat is falling off of the bone (the bone sweetens the soup).

While the meat is cooking, cut the tips and heads off of the okra. Finely slice the okra: don't dice it! Chop your onions, peppers, garlic, celery and parsley.

Add the chicken and the beef to the pot when the meat is almost off the bone. Add tomatoes, onions, green and red peppers, celery and garlic. Continue to cook slowly.

When it's almost ready, add cut corn and crushed tomatoes. Add okra and shrimp in the last ten minutes of cooking. If the shrimp cook too long they will be tough.

This soup should be eaten with white rice.

I was raised on Gumbo; in my house we also called it Okra Soup. Gumbo has been described as the "poor man's meal," or a "Saturday dish," prepared when you emptied your refrigerator at the end of the week. As far as I'm concerned Gumbo is a luxury. It takes all day to prepare (to do it right) and the fresh okra required to make it can be difficult to locate and expensive.

Preface

BY TONI CADE BAMBARA

"Call on the ancestors"—NANA PEAZANT

DOWN IN THE Georgia and Carolina Sea Islands they still tell the story of the Ibos. They say that when the boat brought the Africans in from the big slaving ships, the Ibos stepped onto shore in their chains, took a look around, and, seeing what the Europeans further had in store for them, turned right around and walked all the way home to the Motherland.

Take 1: Eldersay, 1948. Great grandmama, encouraging the mind to leap, taught that we can indeed walk on the water, so long as we know where we're going and why. "Course, fear of sinking stops many folk from taking necessary steps," she'd say. "And too, we're trained in this land to distrust the journey entirely."

Take 2: Literature, 1984. Paule Marshall opens her diasporic novel *Praise Song for the Widow* with her protagonist, Avey Johnson preparing for a journey whose outcome hinges on the tale of the Ibos. Avey, who has bargained away the wealth of her cultural heritage in exchange for a "respectable" life, takes a Caribbean cruise with equally deracinated friends. At sea, a disturbing dream awakes her.

She senses her carefully planned life unravelling. She leaves the ship and embarks on a journey into the past.

The historical, persistent past unleashes its power through an ancient ritual that the women of the island reenact for the ailing Avey. The immediate past, Avey's girlhood in Tatum, South Carolina, unleashes its power through the memory of Great Aunt Cluny telling the tale of the Ibos, which was handed down by Cluny's grandmother, who'd add, "My body may be here, but my mind's long gone with the Ibos."

Through the strength Avey draws from the tale, she learns to read again the cultural codes and signs of her heritage. She reclaims her original name, Avatara—rebirth through memory and revelation. Now centered Avatara envisions a new life's work—warning the assimilated away from eccentricity. She'll haunt office buildings and confront amnesiacs. She'll return to Tatum and conduct tours. "Here," she'll say, indicating a spot near shore. "Here's where the Ibos landed."

Take 3: Cinema, 1991. Julie Dash announces early in *Daughters of the Dust* her stance regarding the great American afflictions, amnesia and disconnectedness. The film begins with three injunctions to remember the past: the *Black Gnostic* is quoted, the Ibo phrase for "remember" is chanted, an elder's hand sculling the waters of time is repeated. It is not long before the Ibo tale is recited and begins to function as both evidence of, and argument for, cultural continuity.

Following the credits, a boat glides down a thick, green river. Standing near the front of the boat is a woman in a long white dress and a large veiled hat. The image is familiar from dominant cinema's colonialism-as-entertainment genre. But we notice that this woman stands hipshot, chin cocked, one arm akimbo. These ebonics signify that filmmaker Dash has appropriated the image from reactionary cinema for an emancipatory purpose. She intends to heal our imperialized eyes.

The boat pulls into shore where a statue—a male African figure, once affixed to the prow of a European slaving ship—bobs in the shallows. The boat docks at Ibo Landing. The year is 1902. We meet a family, the Peazants, at a critical moment: several members have elected to migrate north for better jobs and schooling. Nana, the head of the family has called the Peazants together for a reunion picnic. She performs a ritual of protections against the hazards of "crossing over." She creates an amulet from scraps of the ancestral past: her most potent gris-gris is a clump of her mother's hair, a last minute keepsake the mother yanked from her scalp before she was snatched from Nana, the child, and sold down river.

Rituals and tales are regarded by Haagar, one of the daughters-in-law, as the "hoodoo mess" she wishes to rescue her family from by migrating north. Bilal, a Muslim relation on the island, rejects not the tale but its mythic interpretation. His is a literal reading: the weighted-down Ibos chose death over captivity. But Eula, mother of the Unborn Child, who conarrates the film's story with Nana, draws strength from the tale. And through Eula, the relatives are drawn into a healing circle and mend their rifts.

"I'm trying to give you something to track your spirit with"—NANA PEAZANT

What Dash does with the colonialism is our first signal that *Daughters* is oppositional cinema. The use of dual narration and multiple point-of-view camerawork, rather than a hero-dominated perspective, is our second clue that *Daughters* was conceived outside of Hollywood protocol. Dash's eschewing of a master narrative in favor of a nonlinear, multilayered unfolding—one more in keeping with the storytelling traditions that inform African cinema—is further evidence of *Daughters* Africentric grounding. Dash's demystified and democratic treatment of space positions *Daughters* in progressive world film culture movements that bolster socially responsible cinema—Cuban, Caribbean, African, Philipino/Philopina, Cine Nuova, USA Multicultural Independent. In *Daughters*, the emphasis is on shared space (wide-angled and deep-focus shots in which no one becomes backdrop to anyone else's drama) rather than dominated space (foregrounded hero in sharp focus, others Othered in background blur); on social space rather than idealized space (as in westerns); on delineated space that encourages a contiguous-reality reading rather than on masked space in which, through close-ups and framing, the spectator is encouraged to belive that conflicts are solely psychological not, say systemic, hence, can be resolved by a shrink, a lawyer, or a gun, but not say, through societal transformation.

Dash's decision to cast her film with performers associated with the USA Independent Black Cinema Movement calls our attention to her capsulization of film practices developed since the late 1960s. *Daughters*, then, is a historical marker, independent Black cinema come of age.

A declaration of independence was drafted in 1967 with the overturning of the European/Euro-American, industry-oriented film school curriculum at UCLA by a first wave of students and TAs who were more interested in serving their communities as cultural workers than in training for an industry that maligns and invisibilizes those communities. The UCLA insurrection, dubbed "the L.A. rebellion" by film critic Clyde Taylor, sparked Chicana/o, Native American, Asian American, and Pacific Islander American film movements. And it ushered in as well a new phase of one of the oldest independent filmmaking traditions, the African American.

Within the next decade, several insurgents who participated in an off-campus, student-generated study group produced major works: *Bush Mama* by Hailie Gerima (with Barbara O. Jones—now Barbara-O—and Cora Lee Day, who play Yellow Mary and Nana, respectively in *Daughters*), *Passing Through* by Larry Clark, *Four Women* by Julie Dash, *Killer of Sheep* by Charles Burnett (with Kaycee Moore, who plays Haagar in *Daughters*). Thanks to such people as film historian, critic, producer, distributor, curator, and programmer, Pearl Bowser, a minicircuit of nontheatrical venues was developed for the screening of new films coming from the West Coast, the East Coast, Chicago, and for "race films" of previous eras. Equally important, an audience was developing.

In 1980, several UCLA insurgents who participated in both the aforementioned study group and a student-generated women of color collective were at work: Barbara McCullough, on her first, *Water Ritual #1: An Urban Rite Purification*; Sharon Alile Larkin, on a feature, *A Different Image* with Adisa Anderson, who plays Eli in *Daughters*; Julie Dash, on her third short, *Illusions*. By the time *Illusions* was screened, certain traits were recognizable Dash signatures: virtuosa camerawork—most especially in *Four Women*; communal rather than dominated space—most discernible in *Illusions*; experimental narrative; the privileging of black women characters and their perspectives; an attention to the glamour (in the ancient sense of the word) and sheer gorgeousness of black women; and texts drawn from black women writers—Nina Simone for *Four Women* and Alice Walker for *The Diary of an African Nun* (with Barbara O. Jones). As Dash has remarked in various interviews, it was in this period that she committed herself to producing films about black women at various times in history and first began to think about the project that eventually became *Daughters*.

The power of *Daughters* owes much to both Dash's writing ability and her choice of Arthur Jafa (A.J.) as director of cinemaphotography. A.J. not only questions most generic film conventions, but he questions as well whether the standard of twenty-four-frames-per-second rate is kinesthetically the best for rendering the black experience. A particularly breathtaking moment begins with a deep-focus shot of the beach. In the foreground are men in swallowtail coats and homburgs. Some are standing, others sitting. Two or three move across the picture plane, coattails buffeted by the breeze. They speak of the necessity of making right decisions for the sake of the children. Across a stretch of sand glinting in midground, the children play on the shore in the farground. Several men turn to look at the children. In turning, their shoulders, hips, arms, form an open "door" through which the camera moves; maintaining a crisp focus as we approach the children. The frame rate changes just enough to underscore the children as the future. For a split second we seem to travel through time to a realm where children are eternally valid and are eternally the reason for right action. Then the camera pulls back, still maintaining crisp focus as we cross the sands again and reenter the present, the grownups' conversation reclaiming our attention.

"We all good Women"—EULA PEAZANT

Currently *Daughters* is enjoying cult status. It is not unreasonable to predict that it will shortly achieve the status it deserves—classic. What draws black women in particular to the lengthy movie theater lines again and again is the respectful attention Dash gives to our iconography—hair, cloth, jewelry, skin tones, body language. As though in response to the call made by Abbey Lincoln in the September 1966 issue of *Negro Digest*—in "Who Will Revere the Black Woman?"—Dash composes a woman validation ceremony within a film that has already assured the black woman spectator that we are not, as usual, going to be mugged in the dark.

The ceremony revolves around Yellow Mary. She is financially independent, mobile, sassy, wise, favored by Nana, and able to negotiate her life without having to consider children and husband. What's more, she has a female companion and a "past"—grounds enough to be despised, as she is by several relatives. Eula also "ruint," makes a case for all women whose honor and dignity have been plundered. Eula pulls the mutterers and shaded-eye whisperers into a circle and argues for new standards for judging womanhood and selfhood. "If you love yourself, love Yellow Mary," she pleads.

Perhaps, finally with the breakthrough of *Daughters* into the theatrical circuit, new audiences are developing for the culturally-specific works of filmmakers, producers, directors, and videographers within community media, public television, the independent sector, and the commercial industry.

Partial roll call: Nadine Patterson, Teresa Jackson, Cheryl Dunye, Camille Billops, Juanita Anderson, Claire Andrade Watkins, Pearl Bowser, Monica Freeman, Ada Mae Griffin, Pam Jones.

Julie Dash, Alile Sharon Larkin, Barbara McCullough, O. Funmilayo Makarah, Daresha Kyi, Malaika Adero, Neema Barnett, Rommell Foster, Audrey King Lewis, Beverly Fray, Portia Cobb

Ayoka Chenzira, Jackie Frazier, Louisa Fleming, Elena Featherstone, Zeinabu Irene Davis, Ellen Sumter, Carmen Ashurst, Jean Facey, Fronza Woods, Mary Ester

Francee Covington, (the late) Kathy Collins, Maya Angelou, Alexis DeVeaux, Shauneille Perry, Bess Lomax Hawes, Joanne Grant, Carole Munday Lawrence, Barbara-O, Susan Robeson

Michelle Parkerson, Carrol Parrot Blue, Jesse Maple, Debra J. Robinson, Yvonne Smith, Ruby Bell-Gram, Karma Bene Bambara, Sandra Sharp, Carmen Coustat, Pat Hilliard, Donna Suggs

Cheryl Chisholm, Omola Iyabunmi, Denise Oliver, Portia Marshall, Gay Abel-Bey, Amie Williams, Helene Head, Jean Facy, Aarin Burche, Yvette Mattern, Debbie Allen, Denise Bird, Darnell Martin, Muriel Jackson, Sonya Lynn, Anita Addison

Patricia Khayyam, Melissa Maxwell, Ruby Oliver, Melvonna Ballenger, Cynthia Ealey, Donna Mungen, Audrey Lewis, Michelle Colbert, Hattie Gossett, Linda Holmes, Iileen Sands, Edie Lynch, Lisa Jones, Madeline Anderson, Shirikiana Amia Gerima, Imama Hemeen

Special thanks to John Williams, Kharma Bene Bambara, Jackie Shaka, and Zeinabu Irene Davis for assistance in putting together the (regrettably incomplete) roster.

Toni Cade Bambara is based in Philadelphia where she conducts script workshops at the Scribes Video Center, a media-access facility that helps train community-based organizations to use video for social change.

Making
Daughters of the Dust
BY JULIE DASH

I NEVER PLANNED a career as a filmmaker. As a child growing up in the Queensbridge Housing Projects in Long Island City, New York, I dreamed of some typical and not-so-typical career choices. None of the images I saw of African American people, especially the women, suggested that we could actually make movies. We were rarely even in them. No, I never dreamed of filmmaking when I was little. At that time, I wanted to be in the secretarial pool, typing away and having fun like the women I saw on TV and in the movies. I had no idea that the images I saw didn't depict the real life of working women.

Later, I turned my attention to something much more glamorous—Roller Derby. I was amazed by the motion, speed and power of women flying around the roller rink in competition and combat. Yeah that was going to be me. The Roller Derby queen of New York.

A child's dreams. A young girl's fantasies, shaped by the limitations imposed by my environment. My ambitions, like those of most children growing up in

African American neighborhoods, in projects, in inner cities, were stifled by what I thought possible for me as a black child. My dreams were also molded by the cinema and television stories, where the likes of me didn't even exist.

I don't know if I would have survived the secretarial pool long-term. I did learn some office skills, and at different points in my career as a filmmaker I had to take temporary secretarial jobs in order to eat while I continued making films. As for Roller Derby, the television show didn't last long, and I'm not sure I would have survived that, either.

My introduction to filmmaking began at the Studio Museum in Harlem when I was seventeen. I was just tagging along with a friend who had heard about a cinematography workshop there and thought she could learn to take still photos. We joined the workshop and became members of a group of young African Americans discovering the power of making and redefining our images on the screen.

It was fun. As I became involved in the workshop, I enjoyed it and was drawn more and more to it. I'd found something that was creative and exciting and intellectually challenging, but I still didn't think this could be my work.

I made my first film when I was about nineteen. An animation film about a pimp who goes to an African village and is beaten and dragged out of the village by the people there. It was called *The Legend of Carl Lee DuVall*. I used pictures I had cut out of a *Jet* magazine, glued them to pipe cleaners, and shot them with a super-8 camera. I was really beginning to love filmmaking—but still, when I went to college I initially majored in physical education. I was going to be a gym teacher.

While at City College in New York, a special program, the David Picker Film Institute, was set within the Leonard Davis Center for the Performing Arts. I went there and interviewed because it sounded like fun, and I already had some film experience from the Studio Museum. I was accepted and wound up graduating from CCNY with a degree in film production.

At that point I knew my course was set.

LOS ANGELES

As soon as I finished at CCNY, I moved to Los Angeles. My plan was to get into the UCLA film school. I had read about Charles Burnett, Haile Gerima, and Larry Clark making narrative films out in L.A., and that's what I was interested in. At the time, the West Coast seemed to be more involved with narrative films than the East Coast where a lot of black filmmakers, including myself, were making documentary films.

I was very excited about the prospect of UCLA. Considering my previous work and experience, as well as my degree from CCNY and good recommendations, I was sure I would get in. I didn't…because of a technicality.

Applicants to the film school at UCLA had to submit, among other things, three letters of recommendation. I had been promised these letters by three of my teachers (two of them white and one black). To my surprise however, one of the letters was never sent, and as a result I wasn't accepted. I was stunned.

I was even more hurt when I found out that both of the white professors had sent their letters supporting me. I thought getting into UCLA would be a triumph and an advance not just for me as a young African American, but also for other black filmmakers. Instead, I learned a bitter lesson, one that I would remember throughout my career,

A great part of filmmaking is overcoming various kinds of obstacles. What I learned then was that I would sometimes have to face sabotage, often from "my own people." I would have to feel that pain over and over again. While making, *Daughters of the Dust* I encountered this to an extent that I had never suspected.

After the UCLA rejection, I had to figure out what I would do next. I had no other plan because I had been sure I would be in school. Fortunately, Larry Clark was about to begin shooting his film *Passing Through*. I joined his crew and went out into the California desert. One of the actresses I met on *Passing Through* was Cora Lee Day, whom I would cast years later as Nana Peazant in *Daughters of the Dust*.

Working on a film in the desert helped to heal me. I began to get strong again. And once again I stumbled into the next phase of my training.

One afternoon in Los Angeles, my friend and I heard about grants that were available for filmmakers at the American Film Institute (AFI). We went there looking for the grant applications. It all felt very strange to me, because the atmosphere was so relaxed, and AFI was in this beautiful house in Beverly Hills.

We were standing in the hallway looking lost when this young black man dressed in jeans came down the stairs. He said, "My sister, how can I help you?" I thought the brother must work there, you know, maybe he was the janitor (we are all infected by the stereotypes). I told him that we were there to get the grant applications. He listened, asked some questions, and then gave me some of the best advice I was ever given.

He told me to apply for a fellowship instead of a grant. He said that I should be attending AFI, not jut seeking some small cash to make a short film. I took his advice, applied for the fellowship, and became one of the youngest fellows to attend AFI.

Later I discovered that the young man was Ted Lange; he would later be known as Issac on *The Loveboat*. I also found out that he had been the co-writer on Larry's film *Passing Through*.

I always knew I wanted to make films about African American women. To tell stories that had not been told. To show images of our lives that had not been seen.

The original concept for *Daughters* was a short silent film about the migration of an African American family from the Sea Islands off the South Carolina mainland to the mainland and then the North. I envisioned it as a kind of "Last Supper" before migration and the separation of the family.

Barbaro-O

The idea first began to wander throughout my head about 1975, while I was still at AFI. I was making notes from stories and phrases I heard around my family, and became fascinated by a series of James Van Der Zee photos of black women at the turn of the century. The images and ideas combined and grew.

In 1981, I received a Guggenheim

grant to research and write a series of films on black women. In 1983, I completed my short film, *Illusions*, with Lonette McKee in the lead role as a studio executive who passed for white during World War II. This is also when I began intensive research for *Daughters of the Dust*.

Daughters of the Dust

The stories from my own family sparked the idea of *Daughters* and formed the basis for some of the characters. But when I probed my relatives for information about the family history in South Carolina, or about our migration north to New York, they were often reluctant to discuss it. When things got too personal, too close to memories they didn't want to reveal, they would close up, push me away, tell me to go ask someone else. I knew then that the images I wanted to show, the story I wanted to tell, had to touch an audience the way it touched my family. It had to take them back, take them inside their family memories, inside our collective memories.

Two young cast members at rest.

Soon I was off, running faster and faster, trying to find more and more information that would allow me to uncover this story. I spent countless hours in the Schomburg Center for Research in Black Culture in Harlem reading and looking at images from old newspapers, magazines, and books. I went to the National Archives in Washington, D.C., as well as to the Library of Congress and the Smithsonian Institution. UCLA also has a wonderful research library that provided much needed information. And finally I went to the Penn Center on St. Helena Island, off the coast of South Carolina.

The research was fascinating. In fact, if I were not making films, I would probably be glad to spend the rest of my life digging around libraries. I learned so much about the history and experiences of African American people. One of the most fascinating discoveries I made was of the existence of over 60,000 West African words or phrases in use in the English language, a direct result of the slave trade.

As I poured through the documents, taking notes and developing the story line for *Daughters*, it became clear that a short film would not be large enough for the story. I knew I would have to make a feature. There was too much information, and it had to be shared.

THE ELLIS ISLAND FOR AFRICANS

The sea islands of the coast of the Carolinas and Georgia became the main drop-off point for Africans brought to North America as slaves in the days of the transatlantic slave trade. It became the Ellis Island for the Africans, the processing center for the forced immigration of millions. It also became the region with the strongest retention of African culture, although even to this day the influences of African culture are visible everywhere in America.

Many of the images seen in *Daughters of the Dust* parallel the action and behavior of African Americans today. For instance, the hand signals given by two of the men in *Daughters* is a reference to the nonverbal styles of communication of ancient African secret societies which have been passed down across thousands of years and through hundreds of generations. Today these forms are expressed in the secrets of fraternities and in the hand signals of youth gangs.

As a young girl growing up, I remember watching young men on a basketball court or at other gathering places, and before they would drink together, they always poured a little on the ground. I always thought that was a strange and funny ritual. Later, during my research for *Daughters*, I discovered the West African ritual of pouring libations, a show of respect to the ancestors, to family and to tradition. As the men on the basketball court would say, "This is for the brothers who are no longer here or couldn't be here today."

In 1984, while I was still writing, my daughter N'zinga was born. Her birth revealed to me the need to see the past as connected to the future. The story had to show hope, as well as the promise that tradition and family and life would always sustain us, even in the middle of dramatic change. N'zinga's arrival in our lives also brought the "unborn child" into the script. I hadn't seen her until I saw my own daughter.

By 1985, most of my research was completed, and I began to write the script for *Daughters of the Dust*. It would go through five complete rewrites and two polishes.

In fact, I even rewrote some of it while shooting.

Although I did most of the primary research myself, I'm indebted to several people who gave me important help along the way, especially Dr. Margaret Washington Creel, Oscar Sims, and Worth Long.

SHOOTING *Daughters of the Dust*

By late 1986, when I was finally ready to begin shooting, I was faced with another problem: financing the film. Originally I thought it could be done for about $250,000. I had some production money from the National Endowment for the Arts, but it was not enough to begin production. I applied for and received several grants, one from the Fulton County Arts Council (GA), another from the Georgia Council on the Humanities, and another from Appalshop, Southeast Regional Fellowship (SERF). But by the standards of feature productions, it was still not enough, and I soon realized that I would just have to begin, and hope that more money would come when we had something to show.

I knew that it would be difficult to get other people to understand the vision of this unusual film. I knew it would be different from the films most people were used to, and there weren't many people willing to invest in an "untraditional" black movie.

I needed to create on screen what I had in my mind. I knew exactly what it should look like. After hours and days of discussion with Arthur Jafa (A.J.) my coproducer and director of photography, I was confident that we could capture exactly the feelings and memories I wanted to invoke in the mind of the audience. If I could show people a piece of this—literally, give them a piece of my mind—I was sure that I could raise enough money to finance the film. With the grant monies available, and after scraping together unused film stock from friends like Charles Burnett, I decided to shoot a sample of the film.

In the summer of 1987, I took a crew of ten and four cast members, Adisa Anderson, Barbara-O, Alva Rogers and VertaMae Grosvenor (who also served as a technical adviser) to St. Helena Island to shoot for five days. While there, I also conducted screen tests for Unborn Child.

After the initial shooting, we returned to Atlanta, once again broke, and faced the dilemma of trying to find money to edit the sample.

I began to do small projects for various organizations, like the National Black Women's Health Project (the people at NBWHP were extremely supportive of my work and very helpful), and put all of my earnings, beyond basic living expenses, toward editing the sample. Finally, after several months, it was ready to show.

Daughters of the Dust

With a completed script, a sample, and a filmography of my previous work, we renewed our search for funds. I had also revised the budget, based on our experience on St. Helena, and knew that we would actually need around $800,000 to complete the film. We sent packages to a variety of American and European sources. The responses were as interesting as their sources were varied.

Hollywood studios were generally impressed with the look of the film, but somehow they couldn't grasp the concept. They could not process the fact that a black woman filmmaker wanted to make a film about African American women at the turn of the century—particularly a film with a strong family, with characters who weren't living in the ghetto, killing each other and burning things down. And

Cheryl Lynn Bruce

there weren't going to be any explicit sex scenes, either. They thought the film would be unmarketable. They believed that they knew better than we did about what moved black people. They figured it would be a pretty, artsy European sort of film that no one would come to see. Every major studio either passed on it or didn't respond at all.

We didn't do much better in Europe. Most of the European sources couldn't understand what we were trying to do any better than their Hollywood counterparts. One told us the film sounded too much like a typical American film. Another said it was too radical in its concept for their audience. Still others said perhaps next year, if we were still looking for funds by then.

Our most sympathetic response came from the New York-based organization, Women Make Movies Too, which held a benefit fundraiser in 1987. They raised $5,000 for the production. But these funds, as badly needed as they were, only covered the expenses of sending out all the samples. It was beginning to look like we had exhausted all our sources, when a break came that sent us flying into production.

In 1988 I was attending the PBS Rocky Mountain Retreat in Utah. There I met a woman named Lynn Holst, who happened to be director of program development for American Playhouse. Lynn was interested in the project and we spent many hours discussing it. I liked her immediately, and felt that even if nothing came out of our meetings in terms of funding, I'd made a friend. Well, I was rewarded twice. I did make a friend, *and* American Playhouse wound up providing most of the money for *Daughters of the Dust*. Finally, we would be able to make the film.

We entered a two-phase process with American Playhouse. The first was to rework and develop the screenplay even further. We added dialogue and some additional scenes. During this process, I worked closely with Lynn, and I think we learned a lot from each other. Unfortunately, a lot of what we added to the script was ultimately lost due to time and budget constraints.

The second phase was production. American Playhouse insisted we shoot a union film. (We found out later that we didn't have to.) This is often an unfortunate dilemma for independent filmmakers, who want to respect the unions, but

Setting up the "Ride Away" shot.

are rarely able to afford to complete a film in accordance with union guidelines. We wound up striking a deal with the Screen Actors Guild (SAG) under a special contract for minority, low-budget projects. Even with the special terms, we started shooting $200,000 over budget.

We entered the second phase in August of 1989. I met Steven Jones, our line producer and production manager, and Pamm Jackson our associate producer, in Beaufort, South Carolina, to scout locations. We planned to begin shooting by October but nature had something else in mind for us.

In those days, of preproduction, I found myself nauseous and easily fatigued. At first I thought that it was the heat and the humidity, until I learned that I was pregnant. I had to quickly make a decision as to what I was going to do. I had two choices—to put off the production for at least another year or to have an abortion. I made my decision to go forward with the filming of *Daughters.* I flew back to Atlanta to have the abortion. This was a painful decision many women have had to face, especially women who must rely on their physical as well as mental stamina to perform professionally. Unfortunately, many women do not have the same options that I had. At least I could still make a choice. *Daughters* would become the child that I would bear that year.

The week we were to start, Hurricane Hugo slammed into the coast of North and South Carolina. We had just moved our production crew to St. Helena when we were told that the island had to be evacuated immediately, that Hugo would come crashing in on us within a matter of hours. We heard the news about four in the afternoon, and by 10:00 P.M. we had packed all of our equipment and were headed back to Atlanta in a long caravan of cars, trucks, RVs, and vans. We would have to wait out the storm. It was not our first obstacle, and I knew it would not be our last.

When Hugo finally finished feasting on the coast, we returned to shoot *Daughters of the Dust.* Fortunately, it had missed our main locations on the islands. Unfortunately, it hit Charleston and other cities, causing severe damage. Part of our good luck was that some of the relief workers who had helped in Charleston came down later to work with us on the film, some as production assistants and some as cast members. Gloria Naylor, the author of *The Women of Brewster Place* and *Mama Day,* lived in the area, and she joined the crew as a production assistant. It was great to meet her and have her on the set.

When we finally began shooting we knew we had only twenty-eight days to complete all the principal photography. Our main beachfront location (Hunting Island) was a one-mile hike to the coast from base camp. Due to environmental restrictions, we couldn't take a four-wheel-drive vehicle on the nature trail or along the coastline, so all the equipment had to be carried in each morning. We also couldn't bring in a generator, so A.J. decided to shoot with natural light—sunlight—only. Therefore we needed to squeeze in as much shooting time every day as the sun would allow. Often we would be in the middle of setting up or shooting a particular scene when the sun would suddenly cast perfect and beautiful light in another spot. We would hurriedly change directions and capture the unscheduled scene with only a moment's notice. Sometimes this would work, sometimes it failed comically; but we kept shooting.

For the most part, the crew and actors all worked in the same spirit, everyone appreciating that we were doing something different, something special. But, there are always those who cannot or will not see what is being done. Two particular incidents stand out as perhaps the most damaging.

After the shooting had already begun, when we couldn't possibly stop or recast, one of the lead actresses felt that she should be paid more money. Perhaps she had heard that the budget was $800,000 and thought that we were underpaying her, or that I or the other producers were making a lot of money. In fact all of us were working practically for nothing. She and some of the others in the cast apparently didn't understand that $800,000 was an extremely low budget and that I would be heavily in debt when the film was finished. She decided to get the union to force us to pay her more money. When I found out what she was up to, I was hurt and angered. I felt that I had been ambushed by someone whose career I was, after all, helping to promote by casting her in a major role in a feature film.

In independent film, we are never able to pay top salaries. None of us are adequately compensated for the work we do, not the writers, the producers, the directors, the crew, the actors, not one. We do it to create the work. We do it to sharpen our skills. We work with the hope that if the film is good, someone will offer us a bigger budget the next time, and then we'll be able to hire and compensate adequately those who sacrificed on the low-budget projects. We work as a community of artists, collaborating to create a work of art. I was wounded, but had to stifle my emotions and get the best performances out of the actors, while trying to keep the crew focused and motivated.

On another occasion, I was confronted one morning by an actor who refused to put on his costume. We were ready to shoot a scene that included him, and for whatever reason, he decided that this was the time to assert the fact that even though I was the director, he was a man and no woman could make him do anything. This man, a Muslim, who had been telling us all about the need for unity among black people, stood there in the middle of the set, in front of the crew, and confronted me, physically. He knew that he could intimidate most people because of his size (about 6'4") and demeanor. I knew that if I backed down from him the entire project would come crashing around me. Any authority or control I had on the set would be completely undermined. We were seconds away from actually fighting, but I made my stand. What he hadn't anticipated was my willingness to take an ass whipping rather than let him take over my film. I was ready to fight. The seconds passed by, full of tension. I could see his eyes searching my face, looking for signs of fear or weakness. The crew and cast all stood frozen, shocked, unsure. Finally, A.J. intervened and the actor took the opportunity to back away and save face. In the end, he knew that he had too much to lose if he attacked me. He put his costume on. I'd won, but secretly I was shaken for days afterward.

Trula Hoosier

A twenty-eight-day shooting schedule for a feature film is incredibly punishing. We were all exhausted from working long hours day after day, in addition to our constant fight with nature. We were in areas heavily infested with mosquitoes and other biting insects, and were often caught in the middle of sudden and violent sandstorms.

But through it all, we kept shooting. We pushed on, all of us, crew, cast, everyone. We became friends, enemies, lovers, coconspirators and family. Toward the end, we ran short of money and had to wrap some of the cast early. But the spirit of the project had infected some so deeply that they stayed on and worked for nothing for days afterward. Adisa Anderson, Bahni Turpin, and Vertamae Grosvenor were some of those who stayed, helping out where they could, and their help was greatly appreciated.

When we finally wrapped the shooting of *Daughters* there was a great sense of relief, and some sadness. We all felt like we had contributed to something special, something new, something important. It would be a while, almost two years, before we would be able to measure the impact of it on an audience, but we knew it would be special.

We gave a party with food and champagne and music. We showed slides of the crew and cast at work and everybody got a kick out of seeing themselves at some pretty funny moments. I was pleased. We were a good group of hardworking film-makers, and in spite of quite a few problems, we had all forged ahead and made something beautiful. As I enjoyed myself at the party, though, my mind began to run ahead anxiously to the next part of the process. The film now had to be edited, but we had no funds for postproduction and were already heavily in debt.

When we got back to Atlanta, I was physically and emotionally exhausted. Not only had I been consumed with the normal grind of directing a feature film, but I had been constantly fighting for money, managing personalities, and worrying about the next wave of fundraising. I also felt guilty about being away from my daughter for so long while I shot the film. Now I would be home for a while, but the pressure and stress did not end. I still had to edit the film.

I set up my living room as an editing room and watched as 170,000 feet of film was unloaded at my house—a mountain of work, an almost unsurmountable task. Keith Ward, Tommy Burns, and Angela Walker did the syncing of the film, and I began editing in January 1990.

I did what I could with whatever money became available. After the first month I brought in Joseph Burton to help with the editing, and later Amy Carey came on board to help complete it. In June, I was fortunate enough to receive a Rockefeller Fellowship for $45,000 which went immediately into the film. The National Black Programming Consortium also contributed money for postproduction. By December we finally had a fine cut. Now it was time to look for a distributor.

Amy Carey, the editor, and I took the fine cut to Los Angeles to begin producing the original music score with John Barnes. We had already scheduled and rescheduled the sound mix, so we had only two weeks to complete the music before the final sound mix. John Barnes worked throughout the Christmas holiday to compose and score seventy-two musical cues for the film.

*N'jia Kai, Second Camera
Operator & Julie Dash*

*A.J., Director of Photography &
Teresa Yarbrough, Production Office
Coordinatior*

*Jim Fielder, Camera Assistant &
A.J., Director of Photography*

*A.J., Director of Photography &
Cheryl Lynn Bruce*

Alva Rogers

Alva Rogers & Trula Hoosier

bell hooks

Eric Mofford, Location Manager &
A.J., Director of Photgraphy

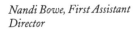

Lorna Johnson, Production Assistant

Alva Rogers & Julie Dash

Nandi Bowe, First Assistant
Director

Tracie Morris, Production Assistant
& A.J., Director of Photography

Bahni Turpin

For the soundtrack of *Daughters of the Dust*, John assembled an impressive collection of musicians and styles to evoke the film's magic and mystery. He used a myriad of instruments, including the synclavier, the Middle Eastern santour, African bata drums and African talking drums, and he successfully mixed synclavier-based percussion with authentic music from Africa, India, and the Middle East.

We wanted to depict various religions—including traditional West African worship rituals, Santeria, Islam, Catholicism, and Baptist beliefs—through musical expression.

John drew from his own spiritual beliefs, which include a respect for astrology, in composing the music. For instance, he wrote the Unborn Child's theme in the key of B, the key of Libra, representing balance and justice. "This character was coming into the world to impart justice, a healing upon her father and her mother and her family." Similarly, he wrote "Nana's Theme" in the key of A representing the Age of Aquarius, or the new age that was imminent for Nana's family.

The closing theme, called the "Elegba Theme," was written in the key of Taurus, D sharp (or E flat). John told me, "It is the key of the earth, the key ruled by love." The lyrics, "Ago Elegba . . . show the way, Elegba," he says, are about people who are moving forward after having been given love and dignity, and who are now facing the crossroads.

While we were recording the score, we began the final sound mix at Sound Trax Studios in Burbank, California. We recorded at night and mixed during the day. The whole recording session went on for ten continuous days in which we barely slept a wink.

I was certain that now that the film was completed, distribution would not be a problem. It had been hard in the early days to convey in words the idea of this film. But now that it was done, I figured there'd be no more blank looks. They wouldn't have to imagine a film about African American women at the turn of the century. Here it was, right in front of them. I was wrong. All of the distribution companies turned it town.

I was told over and over again that there was no market for the film. The distributors talked about the spectacular look of the film and the images and story being so different and thought-provoking, yet the consistent response was that there

Hands of Young Nana holding Sea Island soil.

(above) Yellow Mary and Trula arrive, accompanied by Myown and Iona.

(right) The Peazant Women, shocked by Yellow Mary's arrival.

Diva confrontation: Hagaar and Yellow Mary

(above) Nana examines Yellow Mary's St. Christopher Charm.

(previous spread) Eula looks on as Eli walks on water at Ibo Landing.

(above) Close-up

(above) Viola"s mother sits for photograher.

(right) Viola's mother instructs young family member.

Eula, Trula, and Yellow Mary

was "no market" for this type of film. Again, I was hearing mostly white men telling me, an African American woman, what my people wanted to see. In fact, they were deciding what we should be allowed to see. I knew that was wrong. I knew they were wrong.

One of the ongoing struggles of African American filmmakers is the fight against being pushed, through financial and social pressure, into telling only one kind of story. African Americans have stores as varied as any other people in American society. As varied as any other people in the world. Our lives, our history, our present reality is no more limited to "ghetto" stories, than Italian Americans are to the Mafia, or Jewish Americans are to the Holocaust. We have so many, many stories to tell. It will greatly enrich American filmmaking and American culture if we tell them.

In order to secure distribution for *Daughters* I decided to start showing it on the festival circuit. The fist one we were able to present at was the prestigious Sundance Festival in Utah, in 1991.

The film was well received, as we thought it would be, and won the festival's award for best cinematography. I was very happy, not only for the success of the film, but for the recognition given to A.J. for his work as cinematographer.

I took it to festival after festival, from January through September 1991. At the Black Light Festival in Chicago, *Daughters* sold out every showing. I went to Germany, to the Munich Film Festival and the film got a tremendous response there. Everywhere we took it, whether it was the Toronto Film Festival, the London Film Festival, or the Festival of Women in Spain, the response was the same. *Daughters of the Dust* provoked the audience. Most liked it, some did not. But it provoked them, and that made me see that I had created something important, a film that caused its audience to think and react and come to grips with their own memories.

During this period I was commissioned by Alive From Off Center to direct *Praise House*, a performance film featuring the Urban Bush Women. I was glad to do the work; I was always moved and intrigued by the work of the Urban Bush Women. Also, the money helped me pay off my debt.

Finally, in September 1991, a small company operating out of New York, Kino International, agreed to act as the distributor for *Daughters of the Dust*. I was relieved, but concerned, because they only agreed to distribute the film on a staggered schedule throughout 1992. I had hoped for a simultaneous release in key markets throughout the United States. I think it is important that African American filmmakers get maximum exposure for their films during the initial release period. If not, they're often pulled before the audience has a chance to find them. This is what happened to Charles Burnett's excellent film, *To Sleep with Anger*.

The other concern that I and other African American filmmakers are faced with is the amount of money that the distributor will spend on prints and advertising. When a film is released on a staggered schedule, it often means a very small budget for promotion, thereby limiting the exposure and the potential revenues of the film.

In this case, however, I was lucky and Kino International made a big push for the opening of the film. They also had the wisdom to hire a new African American public relations firm, KJM 3, to arrange publicity for the film. KJM 3 worked hard, and I soon found myself swamped with requests for interviews. Suddenly, I was appearing in national magazines and newspapers all across the country.

Daughters of the Dust opened January 15, 1992, at the Film Forum in New York. It sold out every show. The day of the opening the Coalition of One Hundred Black Women of New York gave a fashion show and reception in support of the film. I was overwhelmed. People were asking me how it felt to be the first African American woman filmmaker with a feature film in theatrical release. It was a thought that had never crossed my mind. I had always considered myself one of a community of some very talented, powerful women filmmaker—women such as Neema Barnett, Ayoka Chenzira, Zeinabu Irene Davis, and Michell Parkerson. Now people were saying, "Oh you're Julie Dash."

Daughters of the Dust had finally made it to the screen. As I watched people file out of the theater on opening night, I felt all kinds of emotions. I was happy to see my work so well received; I was moved by the emotion on the faces of the people, especially older African Americans; I was proud to be contributing to the growing power of African American filmmakers, telling the stories of our people; and I was relieved that the voices of our women were finally being heard. But I didn't bask in the success of *Daughters* for too long. By the time it opened, I was already promoting the next film.

Dialogue

BETWEEN BELL HOOKS AND JULIE DASH

APRIL 26, 1992

BELL: I'm here in Atlanta, Georgia, talking with filmmaker Julie Dash. Hi, Julie Dash girl!

JULIE: Hi, bell hooks. How ya doing?

BELL: I'm doing good. The first thing that I wanted to talk about was the whole question of ethnography in relation to *Daughters of the Dust*. When it comes on the screen, it says, "At the turn of the century, Sea Island Gullahs, descendants of African captives, remained isolated from the mainland of South Carolina and Georgia. As a result of their isolation, the Gullah created and maintained a distinct, imaginative, and original African American culture." That definite citing of history evokes the notion of documentary, and because of the film's ethnic material, I think it can be seen as having some qualities of ethnographic film.

JULIE: Right. I put that flag, or prologue, in after the film had been edited, after it was completed, because a lot of people did not know anything about the Gullah, or Geechee culture. They did not even know anything about the Sea Islands of the South. So we did that to help them along, to give them some background history before we jumped into the story. I wasn't really thinking in terms of an ethnographic film. I was drawing upon what I had experienced watching films by Spencer Williams, films from the 1930s, like *The Blood of Jesus* and *Go Down Death*. Those are dramatic, religious kinds of stories, but they also had this "ethnographic," I guess you could call it, quality to them.

Daughters of the Dust

BELL: I didn't mean to suggest that I felt *Daughters* had an ethnographic quality. But I felt that one could see links between it and certain ethnographic films. It seems to me that part of what *Daughters of the Dust* does is construct for us an imaginative universe around the question of blackness and black identity—which you do, in fact, situate historically. I mean, in your interview in *Transition* with Houston Baker (November, 1992), you say that you wanted to bring "a basic integrity to the historical events."

JULIE: Yes.

BELL: And I think it is that effort on your part that creates a tension between the notion of history and a kind of mythobiography.

JULIE: Yes, I would agree with all of that. But I would just like to add that I think one of the problems that some people have with *Daughters of the Dust* is that they get a lot of new information in the film. With most films you get one or two pieces of new information. And whenever new information is being presented, I think audiences tend to put themselves in the position of "Oh, so I'm like the student here. If this is a learning-teaching situation, then this must be a documentary." They immediately revert to being children in school, rather than adults who are being offered something they hadn't known before. I also think this is something that has to do with information about black people, people of color. When there is a layering of new information, it is thought to be a documentary presentation rather than a dramatic film with a whole lot of stuff in it that a lot of people just didn't know before.

BELL: Well, that's interesting, because I like experimental fiction—like the work of the Sri Lankan Canadian writer, Michael Ondaajte, *Coming Through Slaughter*, which is more or less about the life of Buddy Bolden; or Theresa Hak Chae, a Korean writer. And both of these people experiment with bringing certain factual information into a kind of mythopoetic context.

Part of the challenge of *Daughters of the Dust* is that it brings us what could be called ethnographic details, though in fact it's set within a much more poetic, mythic universe. I would like you to talk some about your sense of myth and history.

JULIE: It's interesting that you say mythopoetic, because *Daughters of the Dust* is like speculative fiction, like a *what if* situation on so many different levels.

Like *what if* we could have an unborn child come and visit her family-to-be and help solve the family's problems.

What if we had a great-grandmother who could not physically make the journey north but who could send her spirit with them.

What if we had a family that had such a fellowship with the ancestors that they helped guide them, and so on.

Myth, of course, plays, a very important part in all of our lives, in everyone's culture. Without myth and tradition, what is there? So there is the myth of the Ibo Landing, which helped sustain the slaves, the people who were living in that region.

BELL: Tell people what that myth is.

JULIE: Okay. The Ibo Landing myth—there are two myths and one reality, I guess.

Ibo captives, African captives of the Ibo tribe, when they were brought to the New World, they refused to live in slavery. There are accounts of them having walked into the water, and then on top of the water all the way back to Africa, you know, rather than live in slavery in chains. There are also myths of them having flown from the water, flown all the way back to Africa. And then there is the story—the truth or the myth—of them walking into the water and drowning themselves in front of the captors.

I was able, in my research, to read some of the accounts from the sailors who were on the ship when supposedly it happened, and a lot of the shipmates, the sailors or other crew members, they had nervous breakdowns watching this. Watching the Ibo men and women and children in shackles, walking into the water and holding themselves under the water until they in fact drowned.

And then interestingly enough, in my research, I found that almost every Sea Island has a little inlet, or a little area where the people say, "This is Ibo Landing. This is where it happened. This is where this thing really happened." And so, why is it that on every little island—and there are so many places—people say, "This is actually Ibo Landing"? It's because that message is so strong, so powerful, so sustaining to the tradition of resistance, by any means possible, that every Gullah community embraces this myth. So I learned that myth is very important in the struggle to maintain a sense of self and to move forward into the future.

BELL: It's interesting that whenever an artist takes a kind of mythic universe and infuses it with aspects of everyday reality, like the images of women cooking, often the cinema audience in this society just isn't prepared. So few of the articles that I've read about *Daughters of the Dust* talk about the mythic element in the film, because, in fact, there is this desire to reduce the film to some sense of historical accuracy. It is relevant for moviegoers to realize that you did ten years of research for this film—but the point was not to create some kind of documentary of the Gullah, but to take that factual information and infuse it with an imaginative construction, as you just told us.

Yesterday I interviewed a young black woman, a graduate student, and she said, "This was our paradise that we never had." And I found that exciting, because she wasn't relating to the film, as "Dash was trying to create this ethnographic memory." No, you were giving us a mythic memory.

JULIE: Right, because life on the Sea Islands was very hard. Most people didn't live very long. There are extreme changes in temperature there, and life was very harsh. But the particular day that I presented in the story was a day that every family member would never forget. And I think that even within our lives—which are also very difficult—we remember these kinds of ceremonies and family dinners as being something very special, and that's all you remember. Of course it becomes mythologized.

BELL: And there is a certain hyperbolic quality when we retell stories.

JULIE: Exactly. They become more so.

BELL: They become larger than life, and to some extent what you do is create a film where many of the images are larger than life. And the object isn't to create any kind of accuracy. I was very moved by what you said in the *Transition* interview about indigo and your sense, as an imaginative creative artist, that you wanted to have something atypical be seen as the scars of black people.

JULIE: I worked with Dr. Margaret Washington Creel, who is an expert on the Gullah. She was my historical adviser on the project, and she reminded me that, of course, indigo was very poisonous and all that, but that the indigo stain, the blue stain, would not have remained on the hands of the old folks who had worked the indigo processing plant. And I explained to her, that yes, I did understand that fully, but I was using this as a symbol of slavery, to create a new kind of icon around slavery rather than the traditional showing of the whip marks or the chains. Because we've seen all those things before and we've become very calloused about them. I wanted to show it in a new way.

BELL: I think of Victor Slosky's notion of "defamiliarization," where you take what may be an everyday image and you present it in such a way that people have to think twice. As a spectator, when I saw that I immediately thought about the permanent imprinting of wounds in flesh. But I didn't have to pause and ask, "But is this real?" because that isn't the point.

I think one of the major problems facing black filmmakers is the way both spectators and, often, the dominant culture want to reduce us to some narrow notion of "real" or "accurate." And it seems to me that one of the groundbreaking aspects of *Daughters of the Dust*, because it truly is a groundbreaking film, is its insistence on a movement away from dependence on "reality," "accuracy," "authenticity," into a realm of the imaginative.

Could you say more about your sense of memory? What does it mean, if you're not going to work in a documentary form, to emphasize so much the idea of memory and time?

[31]

JULIE: After I concluded my research on *Daughters*, I sat back and digested all of that information and said, okay, I want to maintain historical events and issues and the integrity of this region, of these people. But I also want to do something very different, and that's where we get into the poetic thing. I want to show black families, particularly black women, as we have never seen them before. I want to touch something inside of each black person that sees it, some part of them that's never been touched before. So I said, let me take all of this information that I have gathered and try to show this family leaving a great-grandmother in a very differ-ent way. And that was when I realized that I could not structure it as a normal, Western drama. It had to go beyond that. And that's when I came up with the idea of structuring the story in much the same way that an African griot would recount a family's history. The story would just kind of unravel. This very important day would unravel through a series of vignettes, if you want to call them that. The sto-ry would come out and come in and go out and come in, very much the way in Toni Cade Bambara's work one character would be speaking to another and then it goes off on a tangent for several pages and then she brings it back and goes out and back again.

I remember learning about poetry in school; the teacher said, "Well, what makes poetry good is that poets will say things using words that you use every day but they say them in a way that you have never heard it said before. And then it means so much more."

BELL: And that's like the concept of defamiliarization. I think that it's precisely because we are not familiar with this form that the criticisms people have brought to bear on this film have been severely limited. I mean, very few people have seen this as a political film. Looking at it for the fifth or sixth time—I was thinking about Barbara Harlow's book on resistance literature, where she looks at literature from North Africa, Palestine, and many other Third World countries that are struggling for liberation—it struck me that in our efforts to decolonize and liber-ate ourselves as black people, or any oppressed group globally, we have to redefine our history, and our mythic history as well. Because *Daughters* does this in such an incredible way, it creates a new kind of art film because it clearly can be seen as an art film, but also as a progressive political intervention. There are images of black people in this film, images of us as we've never seen ourselves on the screen before.

JULIE: But it's not just how the scenes are set up. We could get more specific and say it's the way the cameras are placed. Where the camera is placed, the closeness. Being inside the group rather than outside, as a spectator, outside looking in. We're inside; we're right in there. We're listening to intimate conversation between the women, while usually it's the men we hear talking and the women kind of walk by in the background. This time we overhear the women. So it's all from the point of view of a woman—about the women—and the men are kind of just on the periphery.

But I want to get back to what we were discussing about showing, depicting historical moments in a very different way, in a way that has more meaning. One of the scenes that did not, unfortunately, make it into the film because of time—and there are so many of them—is a flashback to a period of slavery when Nana Peazant's mother cuts off a lock of her hair and puts it inside of a small baby quilt for the young baby Nana, who has been taken away from her and sold into slavery. The mother would send the quilt on to that plantation and when the child was old enough she'd be able to look in her own baby blanket and find a lock of her mother's hair. And sometimes that was the only thing that we had to share with our children or with our husbands and wives. They would send hair by messenger from plantation to plantation. And you know, during my research, I was brought to tears many times. I mean, if all you ever saw of your mother was a lock of her hair, that's all you had, and that's what you had to hang on to for the rest of your life…

I wanted to show that, but it had to be something more than just cutting the hair off or opening up an old package and finding a piece of ancient hair in there. I wanted to show what it really meant to lose a child. And I didn't really fully understand this until after I had a child—since it took so long to write *Daughters of the Dust*, I'd had a child in that ten-year period.

Anyway, I wrote a scene in which you see a woman who cuts off a lock of hair and places it within the baby blanket, but instead of seeing the traditional tears flow from her eyes, we had milk tears flowing from her engorged breasts. Because when you take a baby from a mother, a newborn, the mother continues to produce milk. That doesn't stop for two or three weeks, and the milk leaks. And if she thinks about her baby, the milk leaks even faster. So we had a special-effects gadget rigged up, and we panned down from the woman's face and you see droplets of milk seeping through her dress and falling onto the ground. She is weeping milk tears for the child that has been taken from her rather than just boo-hooing and crying salt-water tears. I really hated not being able to include that in the film because for me, no matter how much I read about it or heard about it, I really could not fully understand what it meant to have a child or an infant taken from you.

BELL: But your point is to evoke that emotionality, that emotional psychic universe, and not necessarily the historical universe. I think historians, people who have written about the Gullah, look at your film and think, "She read me. She took that from me." Can you just talk a little bit about that process of research?

JULIE: Well, the research was a combination of oral histories that I gathered from families, from friends of my family, as well as oral histories that had been taken a long time ago, by the WPA before World War II. There were also letters and lots of other written sources.

But I think when you're talking about folklore—about names, poetry, myths, traditions, notions—when you're dealing with the culture of a people, you're going to find a lot of overlap. A lot of people had this work in their books because they either researched it, heard it. . .

BELL: And so it's repeated?

JULIE: Exactly, yeah.

BELL: So people may think they're seeing their work when it may not be *their* particular work.

JULIE: Right. It might be something that my father said to me over and over again, like the name "Peazant." He used to always talk about Peazant, Peazant, and so I name the family Peazant because it was a very interesting name. And it also sounded like 'peasant.'

BELL: It's sort of like my grandmother's favorite saying—she'd say, "Play with a

Alva Rogers and Barbara-O in demo reel, shot in 1987.

[35]

puppy, he'll lick you in the mouth." And I always figured that was hers, that it belonged to her. And that was where I learned it. And then, later, when I used it a lot, people would say to me, "Oh, did you get that from so-and-so's book?" when I hadn't even read so-and-so's book.

JULIE: Right. A lot of people, they remember Toni Morrison's *Beloved* when they see *Daughters*. We shot the demo reel for it in '87 and then we went back and shot the rest of the film in '89. So we were shooting in the summer of '87. I believe we began shooting before *Beloved* went to press.

BELL: And then, for example, the film's focus on Islam reminds us that, indeed, African Americans draw upon numerous religious traditions. It just so happens that the focus on Islam in the film coincides with the rebirth of nationalism and a renewed focus on Black Muslim identity in America. Some people may see you as drawing on trends in the culture right now, but in fact your thinking about those things predates the resurgence of that interest.

JULIE: Oh, absolutely.

BELL: Somebody recently raised the question with me—were you a black nationalist, or were you an Afrocentric? And I myself wasn't sure why they were gleaning that from the film. I suppose for them it was your focus on Islam. So, could you talk a little bit about that question? What you wanted to show in terms of religion in the film.

JULIE: Well, when I came to the project, I assumed that I already knew a lot about it from my family and from the little research I had done early on. But as I got deeper and deeper into it, I learned a hell of a lot. For instance, I learned about Bilal Muhammed. Actually, he lived earlier than the time of my story. He was in the Sea Islands during slavery, but by the turn of the century, his five daughters who were also Muslim, were still carrying on the tradition of Islam. He was an actual person, a Muslim, and his diaries and his papers are on permanent exhibition at the Smithsonian Institution in Washington. He had been a boy of twelve when he was taken from the Sudan, which shows that the African slave trade was more widespread than we thought—because he had memories of growing up in

[36]

Sudan. He was also fluent in French, having worked as a slave in the West Indies before being brought to the Sea Islands. And he never stopped practicing his faith. As a slave in the Sea Islands he prayed five times a day. People thought he was just an odd fellow, but it really goes to show the persistence of tradition.

BELL: Wow!

JULIE: So it was very important for me to include this man in the story, even though I knew *actually* that he was living and practicing his faith in the 1800s. I wanted him to be a part of this day too, to include him because he meant so much to me. No one else has dealt with him to this point. Strange…

BELL: Yes. I was also interested in Viola's sense of Christianity in the film, as a kind of counterpoint to Islam. History for her begins not with what has happened in the slave past or what is happening on the islands, but at that moment of crossover. And in that sense, she represents a kind of premodern figure for me, because she's the one that says, essentially, "When we cross over to the mainland we are going to have Culture." That's capital-C culture.

JULIE: Exactly. Viola is someone who hides within Christianity. She hides her fears, her lack of self-esteem, her womanhood, within the cloak of the Christian missionary. But it's interesting that this particular character chooses to be a Baptist, because Baptist worship is so close to the ecstatic seizures evoked in lots of West African religions. So a lot of African American people will hide within this Baptist religion, but they're really practicing the same thing. They're just hiding their gods, hiding their rituals within Christianity, which for them was modern.

BELL: I think she definitely stands—as does Haagar—for a force of denial, denial of the primal memory. I keep thinking about violation when I think about Viola because it seems to me that if she had her way, she would strip the past of all memory and would replace it only with markers of what she takes to be the new civilization. In this way Christianity becomes a hidden force of colonialism.

JULIE: Uh-huh, exactly.

BELL: The film really touched upon the question of domestic colonization and how black people, like Haagar and like Viola internalized a sense of what culture is.

Daughters of the Dust

JULIE: Right. And she brought her photographer with her to document "them." She pays the photographer to come document her family. He being a part of the "talented tenth," a scientist. But I see the character of Mr. Snead as having a secret mission. He has another agenda. He's going to take pictures of these very, very primitive people and go back and have a showing of what he's photographed, you know. For me, he also represents the viewing audience.

BELL: In that sense, *Daughters of the Dust* becomes a kind of critical commentary on the ethnographic film, because one might talk about Viola as a kind of contemporary anthropologist—the ethnographer, and Mr. Snead as the ethnographic filmmaker, and the film explodes that. It disrupts their vision and it says that, in fact, she can't really give up on those traditions of the past, and still be a whole self. That's so explicit in the film.

It seems to me that we're touching upon aspects of the film that have so far gone unacknowledged by the critics, so I want us to talk a little bit about why it is that there is no fully developed, critical entity that can address a film like *Daughters of the Dust*? Let's go back to the first white male critic's response. I forget his name; it was after the Sundance Festival.

Julie Dash and with Unborn Child in between scenes.

JULIE: Oh, the *Daily Variety* article, by Todd Carr.

BELL: And what was his point?

JULIE: He wrote that the film didn't explain enough about the Gullah people, their culture, their religious traditions. Responding to this kind of concern, I've trained myself not to go too deep into explaining things about *Daughters*. I'll often cloak things, because a lot of people will just never understand, and sometimes if you give people just a little bit of information it's worse than giving them the whole thing. So I have been cutting short my responses.

BELL: So I hear you saying that part of the danger of being a ground-breaker, in some sense, is that you don't have the time or the energy to educate every critic as to how they might approach this film. I often read your interviews, and I sense that you are repressing a lot because you don't want to have to go through that education process. But, in fact, a lot of the time the result is a critique like Carr's where he says, "But for a work so heavily into its own ethnicity, one is left with any number of unanswered questions relating to Gullah history. . . . Regardless of the extent of research, [the film] refuses to satisfy on a documentary level."

Now this is the type of review that really shows to me a complete misunderstanding of the critical project in *Daughters of the Dust*, because he's simply imposing on you a documentary mission that you yourself did not take on.

What I want to ask you, then, is: Should there have been greater discussion of the need for a different kind of critical spectatorship before the film appeared?

JULIE: Right after *Daughters* screened at the Sundance Film Festival, we had a screening in New York for cultural critics, writers, filmmakers, theorists. We had a screening at the Anthology Film Archives. We provided a press kit that was very very thorough in terms of my intent, the intent of the production designer, et cetera. It also included character descriptions and symbols and everything that's in the film in order to acquaint the uninitiated, so to speak, to what the story is about and what it really means. Beyond that, I don't know any other process, any other way of making it clear to reviewers.

BELL: One of the major ways in which *Daughters of the Dust* intervenes powerfully in the history of feature-length filmmaking about black people is by requiring people to interrogate the Eurocentrc biases that have informed our understanding of the African American experience. I mean, we've never been taught, most of us, in any history class that black people had different languages, had different religious practices, et cetera. So, to some extent, the film does represent that challenge to the critic of any race. When you said earlier that you wanted black people to see themselves, ourselves, in a new way, my understanding was that for any other spectator the challenge is to see blackness in a new way. I don't think you

[39]

meant to suggest that you conceive of the audience of this film as being solely black people, or, for that matter, solely black women.

JULIE: No, I didn't. I wanted black women first, the black community second, white women third. That's who I was trying to privilege with this film. And everyone else after that.

BELL: To de-center the white patriarchal gaze, we indeed have to focus on someone else for a change. And in this sense, again, the film takes up that group that is truly on the bottom of this society's race-sex hierarchy. Black women tend not to be seen, or to be seen solely as stereotypes. And part of what *Daughters* does is de-center the usual subject—and that includes white women—and place at the center of our gaze a group that has not been at the center. To quote Macolm X, from *The Ballot and the Bullet*, "Let's see them with new eyes." And I think the challenge of *Daughters of the Dust*, for any spectator, is to be able to look at blackness with a new eye.

JULIE: And for about two hours too, and then to be comfortable with that. And I've said, often, that I think a lot of people are severely disturbed by the film because they're not used to spending two hours as a black person, as a black woman...

BELL: Girlfriend, talk about it.

JULIE: Film is hypnotic. When you go into a cinema you extend your belief for hours and you become who or what's up on the screen. And I think that for a lot for white males, and black males too, they love to see films that are about what they don't want to be, have never been, are afraid to be, or could only be for two hours. The "New Jack" type of film. They get to go there and assume the personality of the characters on the screen for two hours, then get up and go back to their normal safe lives. A lot of people couldn't do that for *Daughters of the Dust*. Some people just go flying out of the audience. I mean, I've seen men run out of the theater.

BELL: The film requires that we be empathetic with a group in our society that even black women have been taught not to be empathetic with. And we can think about that in terms of the spectacle of the Thomas hearings when, whether one is pro–Anita Hill politically or not, you can still feel that she demands some degree of justice if she was sexually harassed. But the idea that so many black women disassociated from her image...,

JULIE: And went on to him, yeah, because "he had to be right because he's a black male," or "it's about unity and we have to stick behind him."

BELL: I mean, the fact is, we're never going to see a break with the stereotype if someone does not intervene and challenge us to think and feel differently about the black female image. I mean, as long as people are comfortable with the black woman as prostitute, mammy, or slut, and those are the only images people can embrace, what has to take place before they can embrace alternative images?

JULIE: Or a black person being addicted to something. In this country, every black person is addicted to something. Otherwise, they don't have a story.

BELL: But what has to take place? What conditions? I interviewed a black woman yesterday who summed up what so many black women I've interviewed feel when she said, "All my life I have experienced my absence on the screen. Nothing that I could relate to." So I think that psychically, a lot of black women viewers were prepared for the radical visual and aesthetic intervention that *Daughters* makes. Because so many of them said to me again and again, in almost the same words, "I was so starved for those

Scene from 1987 demo reel.

images." And I think that, to some extent, we have to ask, why aren't white women and white men and black men and other groups equally starved for those images? I think part of it is because they passively accept the devaluation and denigration of black womanhood.

JULIE: And they're fed from the first time they lock their eyes onto a television screen, their desires are fully fed. They're satisfied. They see no absence of their presence on the screen. I mean, I'm always asking people, when was the last time you saw a film about a black woman who is a trapeze artist? It's out of the question. When was the last time you saw a film about a black woman flying to the moon, on a rocket ship to the moon? It's like, "What?" And then not have it be something about race or being raped or being addicted or being drunk, or, you know—all of that has to go with it too. Forget about black women having a zest for life, a productive life, successful in whatever they want to accomplish. That's too much.

BELL: I would say that the challenge for the audience is to be able to see and see and see again this film until they acquire the apparatus to embrace it. Because the film is so subversive in its requirement that we look at the black female and the image of black people in general. I don't want to keep emphasizing solely black females, because I do believe that there are also a lot of innovations in the portrayal of black masculinity in *Daughters of the Dust*.

But before we go on to that, it seems to me that another aspect of black psychohistory that you capture in the film that hasn't been captured many other places is the struggle between the agrarian life and the migration to the city. And it seems that part of what the film tries to do is remind us that there indeed was some richness to that agrarian life. I feel that one of the major gaps in our narrative as black people is that no one talks about the psychic loss that black people experienced when we left the agrarian South to move to the industrialized North. The point is, you can't talk about the psychic loss if you don't acknowledge that there was something rich there in that rural, agrarian experience. And it seems to me that a lot of people were deeply moved by *Daughters* precisely because it addressed the agrarian experience of black folk.

I mean, how many films do we see where the black folk are holding dirt in their hands and the dirt is not seen as another gesture of our burden? The fact is that most images of black folk working the land that we see on television, or in traditional cinema, are of "the land as our enemy." Us as laborers, just "beasts of burden," and I think *Daughters* questions that and says, "look at this food, byproduct of the land." Can you talk a little bit about the process of shooting this scene with the food, and those jars that people keep? I keep my jars. I have my great-aunt's jars. I have my aunt Charley's, who was a hairdresser, her green jars that she used to have grease in. The film takes those artifacts of daily life and gives them a power as signs that they have not usually been give in our experience.

JULIE: The bottle trees, positioned outside of the Peazants' shanty, were for protection—protection from malevolent or evil spirits. It's my understanding that each bottle would represent a deceased family member or ancestor. The spirits would radiate goodwill, protection, and luck upon the family's house. Today, we place photos of the deceased on altars we've constructed in our home, or we keep photo albums of our family both living and deceased to find that same warmth.

Dialogue between bell hooks and Julie Dash

I've always been fascinated by the various colored bottles black women keep. They are part of what E. Franklin Frazier describes as our "scraps of memories," where we hold and store things, our specially concocted "hair grease," our secrets, our private things.

Some of the jars in *Daughters*, on the windowsills, on the tables, et cetera, were herbal potions, to be used for medical, cosmetic, or protective purposes. Some of the mixtures were for cooking. Basically, they didn't have a drugstore or a supermarket, so they had to make whatever they needed to survive.

BELL: What about the agrarian experience?

JULIE: Early on I received criticism from people, including a lot of black folk, because they wanted to see this family, the Peazant family toiling in the soil. They wanted to see them working. If they didn't see them physically working, then they didn't understand how they lived, how they had food, how they survived. And I kept telling people, look, you don't work on a Sunday, the day that you're saying goodbye to your great-grandmother.

BELL: Girlfriend, growing up as a Southern black woman, in the 1960s, my family felt that you should not work on a Sunday, no matter how hard you had to work the rest of the week.

JULIE: We couldn't even use a pair of scissors on Sunday.

BELL: We could not wear pants, for a long time. I mean it was some serious legacy of "the day of rest."

[43]

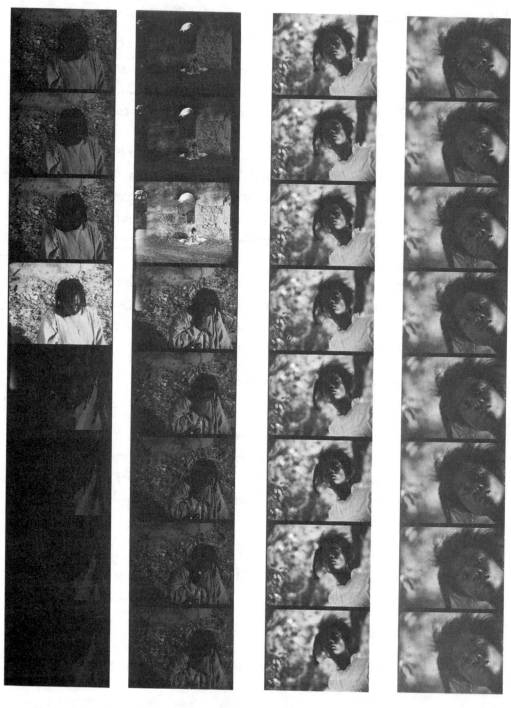

Various scenes from the 1987 demo reel. (left and middle left) Flashback of Nana's mother in shackles. (middle right) Eula looks on as the spirit overtakes Eli. (right) Close-up of Eula.

JULIE: I know. Sunday was serious.

BELL: And you put on your nice clothes, just as people do in the film, and you sat around.

JULIE: But, see, I think because audiences were not used to seeing black folk in their nice dress paying homage to their great-grandmother and not working, not being a beast of burden, they were unable to accept it. No matter what, they still wanted to see someone toiling. They could not accept the fact that this family had food because they were able to sustain themselves from what they planted and what they pulled from the sea. Now, I kept saying this in the dialogue, but still people kept saying, where did they get that food, that beautiful food? The food was there. They pulled it from the land and from the sea. This was a special day. Indeed, they didn't eat like that every day.

BELL: But the very fact that people don't have a way to understand this should remind us of how much we've lost in our understanding of black people and our agrarian past.

JULIE: I think they block it too, because—of course, I wasn't born in 1902, but on feast days, ceremonial days, whenever my Geechee family would get together, this is what our table looked like.

BELL: Well, I mean, I think too that it cuts against the grain of what we have been made to feel poverty is about. Because many of us were raised in Southern backgrounds where there was not a lot of material privilege. But when it came to food, because so much of that food was grown right there, I think of my sharecropper grandfather and all the beautiful food. We would say to Mamaa lot of times, we should take a picture of this table because it looks so beautiful.

JULIE: Right. And every Thanksgiving people would say that. I grew up in the projects. Every Thanksgiving they would say, this table is beautiful, you need to take a picture of it.

BELL: But it seems to me that—

JULIE: So in my mind I did, and I re-created it.

BELL: —that *Daughters* tries to recover the idea that, despite the material hardship that led people to go north or move into the industrialized city, black people did that at a loss. And it seems to me the figure who really addresses that sense of loss most is the Native American.

JULIE: St. Julian Last Child.

BELL: In his relationship to Iona, in the letter that he writes, he so clearly and deeply addresses the sense that something will be lost. Can you talk a little bit about the construction of that character in your imagination?

JULIE: Yes. I wanted, in this film, to speak to the condition of being African American in the Sea Islands at the turn of the century; there were very few Native Americans left in the Sea Islands at that time because, you know, they had all been marched to the reservations in Oklahoma. The Cherokees were some of the original inhabitants of the Sea Islands. So I thought it was important to have one remaining Native American there, and that's why I named him Last Child. He's the last child born of the Cherokee Nation surviving there.

I think in any type of situation where people are forced off the land, there is always some family, some group that stays back, and I see his family as having held back and him the lone survivor. Because the whole film, of course, is about retention, the saving of tradition, persistence of vision. And naturally, since there are no other Native Americans around, he would bond with the black families.

BELL: Or, as we recover our history we know that many Native peoples bonded and intermarried—

JULIE: Absolutely.

BELL: —with African Americans. And we owe books like William Katz's *Black Indians* and—

JULIE: There are certain tribes that were absorbed within the black community to the point where you couldn't distinguish Native American features. They just look African American. And, to my knowledge, that intermarrying has never been depicted on the screen, a Native American and an African American mating, bonding, creating a life together that wasn't just built upon some lust of the moment. I wanted to show that.

BELL: Still, many people have raised the question in my interviews with them about the film: Don't you in some ways reproduce a sort of stock Hollywood image of the Native? Actually, I felt that you tried to subvert the traditional image, because rather than make him a portrait of the illiterate Native American, you actually give him one of the more powerful passages in the film, which is the letter that he writes to Iona where he says things like, "If I lose you I would lose myself," and "Consider the memories." In a sense, that letter and that voice create a kind of tension, because we don't really hear him *speaking* to Iona. So could you talk about your construction of that cinematically.

JULIE: Cinematically? I was going to talk about the writing, which was very difficult, because I wanted it to be very old-sounding, because the style in which we communicate with one another now is very different. I was pulling from old old letters written during the period. We cut out a whole long passage of it, too, in order to save time, but in the beginning it's established that St. Julian Last Child hires someone to write the letter for him. Because in those times we had letter writers. Someone on the island was a good writer, and they would embellish the letter with so many flowery statements. That's why it reads so formally. It reads so, it's bigger than life. It's not just, "Hey Iona, I'll meet you down on the beach because then we could run off together." It's like "Consider the memories, my heart touching yours..." It goes on and on and on.

BELL: Let me interrupt you a minute to say that if one thinks for example, of the portrait of Wind in his Hair in *Dances with Wolves*, there is this one powerful scene which to me was worth seeing all that was trashy in this film, when Wind in His Hair is standing up—

JULIE: On the ledge and they are riding?

BELL: —and Kevin Costner's character has said he's going to leave. And he's standing, he's portrayed—

JULIE: On his horse.

BELL: —on his horse on that ledge, and on the one hand you have the reproduction of the idea of the "noble savage," but on the other hand, it is one of the most
powerful images in the film, of a kind of oneness with nature and the environment
that can be talked about as an aspect of both African and Native American agrarian life. And I thought of St. Julian Last Child in the tree. Where we see him as
though he has, in a sense, emerged out of this tree, out of nature, and exists in har-
mony with it. One of the real problems for those of us who write about Native culture, or African American agrarian culture, is how to break with the romantic
image, but how to also speak the truth of that spirit. Spirit of unity. And it seems to
me that in that one particular moment in *Dances with Wolves* and again and again
in the portrait of the Native, St. Julian Last Child, in *Daughters of the Dust*, there is
that attempt to restore the integrity of being to the idea of being one with nature.

JULIE: It's interesting that you bring that up, because until the last moment I
didn't know whether I was going to use St. Julian Last Child in the tree or the character of Nana Peazant. That scene wasn't written until I got on location, because
when I saw the tree I said, this tree I have got to use, and then, this is how I'm going
to use it. But I didn't know exactly which character was going to be that one in the
tree, sprouting from nature, evoking all the symbols and icons, with the roots at
the bottom and the light and the fog and the sunrise and all that.

BELL: And it is really telling that you would have seen either Nana, who so much
evokes a tradition of African relation to the land, or the Native American.

JULIE: And I chose not to use Nana because I didn't want to worry about her
falling out of that tree.

BELL: Well, it's interesting to me, because in my new book, *Black Look*, I have an
article that is talking about blacks, African Americans, Native Americans, and
Black Indians— about what it means for us as black folk to reclaim that heritage
for our history. When people say to me, "Well, it's a black woman's film," I say,
well, what do you do with the Native American character? Does he have a presence? Does he mean anything for the viewer of that film? We have never seen a

film by a black filmmaker that tried to portray any aspect of Native American culture. Can you name one?

JULIE: No.

BELL: I feel that there is a certain critical denial that takes place, because folks see this film and they know they're seeing stuff that they've never seen before. We know that we have never seen any black filmmaker dare to image anything about Native American culture. To some extent we have bought into the white-supremacist notion that we have no connection to Native Americans.

JULIE: Exactly.

BELL: And our own shame. Many of us were made to feel that we were denying blackness if we claimed that connection. And the film creates that sense, that there was a historical overlap between ideas about nature, divinity, and spirit in those two cultures that made convergence and contact possible. I think *Daughters* tries to show that something which, however flawed, we have no other cinematic example of.

JULIE: Where have you ever seen a Native American win in the end and ride off in glory? When have you ever seen an African American woman riding off into the sunset for love, only, and not escaping?

BELL: And the letter that says—"Our love is a very precious, very fragile flowering of our most. . .

JULIE: ". . .innocent childhood associations. . ."

BELL: ". . .innocent childhood associations." When we talk about the kinds of images and narratives that are progressive in the film, let's focus on some on the reproduction of one real old narrative of black female experience, which is the narrative of rape. One of the things you said in your interview with Houston Baker is that we have seen the physical rape so many times. So talk about why you even chose to work with the theme of rape, and how you saw yourself as doing it in some way that was different.

[49]

JULIE: Okay. Sexual abuse, assault, rape is so much a part of our history that it is a historical fact. But my story revolves around the aftereffects of rape. How an individual deals with being sexually assaulted. How our families deal with this information. How you deal with a loved one—your husband, for instance—because, of course, this kind of assault affects the entire family. It affects your relationships, intimate relationships with your husband or lover.

BELL: When Eli says, "My wife, and some other man was riding her," I just cringe every time I hear that.

JULIE: That was another thing too. I did not want to say the word *rape* ever, so a lot of people are angry because I don't just spell it out. I wanted to say rape without saying R-A-P-E. So the dialogue goes: "She got forced." "Some man was riding her." "Did you tell him? Did you ever tell Eli?" It's the way black women talk about this kind of thing. They don't just come out and say it. Even today, lots of women just don't come out and say it. They work around it.

BELL: One effect of Eli saying, "My wife, and someone else is riding her," is that it allows us to see that there is a connection between his own phallocentricity, his patriarchal sense of ownership, and the mentality of the unknown rapist. And I think there is something about the ambiguity—of course, certainly there is a lot to substantiate that it's a white person—but that ambiguity serves as a kind of critique of the phallocentrism that unites Eli with the rapist. It's Nana Peazant who has to come in and remind him that he does not have to attach himself to this patriarchal fantasy of ownership. Because he has another tradition that he can relate to and which can give him a sense of masculinity that is not disrupted by the actions of the oppressor.

JULIE: Historically, too, African American women never had the luxury of being simply *a woman*. It had to always be so much more: the keeper of secrets, the provider, the nurturer, all of this. We just couldn't be a woman. You're more than that. You're a beast of burden. Someone to breed, this and that. There were always these preconceived assignments that were put on you. You couldn't just be sitting on a veranda sipping a mint julep.

BELL: And I think a part of what the film says is that even in the midst of the denigration of black womanhood, there was the veneration of the black woman as elder. One of the most moving scenes for me in *Daughters* is when Eli and Nana Peazant are at the grave and he says to her, "I really believe you were a goddess." I think it's very much a break with how black women have traditionally been portrayed, that she is not the plump—

JULIE: I had worked with Cora Lee Day almost fifteen years earlier, on Larry Clark's film *Passing Through*. I had to make a choice between Cora and Geraldine Dunston—she plays Viola's mother and is a fine actress—

BELL: Yes. In fact, she was one of my favorite people in the film.

JULIE: But I chose Cora Lee Day for Nana because of her physical appearance, to break with the tradition, the physical image of the "mother" who is going to carry us forward.

BELL: We talked earlier, Julie, about people meeting you or meeting me, you as Julie Dash, me as bell hooks, feminist theorist, and they say to us, "You don't look the way I imagined you would look." People actually say to me, "I thought you were going to be some big, da da da da da." I don't in any way want to denigrate the beauty and power of large black women, but that's something of a stereotype. Now, you're very soft-spoken, as I am, but I think, to some extent there is an association of black female power with size. "Well they've gotta be powerful because they're so big. Because they're so forceful," et cetera. And I think we have to focus on a different kind of power when Nana Peazant is speaking. I mean, it wasn't the power of her voice, she has that voice that just wops you in the film.

JULIE: And the face and the hair. When have we seen our great-grandmothers going to bed at night with their hair tied up looking just like that? When have we seen it on the wide screen?

BELL: How do the images of black women in the film break with stereotypes, transform the image so we are, in fact, called upon to look at black women in different ways?

JULIE: Arthur Jafa, A.J., always says I'm on a mission to redefine how black women look on the screen and what they're doing. I think he's really right and I get teased about it.

BELL: If you would take your film and contrast it with other films you've seen with black women characters, you would see very few other films where the camera really zooms in on black women's faces.

JULIE: And lingers for a period of time. Extreme close-ups and different angles, exactly where the light is caressing them rather than assaulting them. Where the makeup is flawless. Very natural makeup, but flawless. Where the women look attractive, appealing.

bell hooks and A.J.

BELL: And also what I like about *Daughters* is that it didn't claim one black female look, as, "This is attractive and this is not."

JULIE: Right. I wanted to show a whole range.

BELL: How many films even show us more than two black women at a time? So I think it's already a disruption for people to have to focus on that many images of black females at one time, with all those different hair-dos. And we know that a lot of people have crassly said that this is a film about hair. Let's talk about the question of hair.

What do you think about the critics and others who have said that there is too much emphasis on the aesthetic elements of appearance—the hair, the clothes?

JULIE: I think I merely touched the tip of the iceberg compared with what I could have done. I merely touched upon it because we only had $800,000 to work with. And I couldn't get all the people down there that I wanted to. Stylist Pamela Ferrell has a company in D.C. called Cornrows and Company. She pretty much financed her own way down there to work on the film and do the hairstyles, because she had done so much research in Africa. The hairstyles we're wearing now are based upon ancient hairstyles, and there is tradition behind these hairstyles. They mean things. In any West African country, you know, if you are a pre-teen you have a certain hairstyle. If you are in puberty you have another hairstyle. Menopausal, another hairstyle. Married, single, whatever. All of this means something. There is so much meaning to our heritage that just gets overlooked. Like, there was a scene, the scene that I spoke about with Nana's mother cutting off the hair and her weeping the milk tears: her mother's face was covered with tattoos. We researched that. Her face was covered with tattoos. Another scene where the African—it's a flashback scene where I have some of the earliest African members of the Peazant family dancing, we see the scarification on their arms and faces. And another scene that we didn't get a chance to shoot was the family hairbraider braiding the map of their journey north, in the hair design, on a woman's head.

I grew up in New York. People still wrapped their hair. People wore big braids. They wore cornrows. They wore the Madagascan hairstyle that I saw—you know, that was placed upon Viola's mother's head. All of these things I grew up with in New York.

BELL: But in terms of cinematic portrayal, we have had very few images that suggest there is any beauty or pleasure to be found in our hair. And I agree with you that my experience with hair while growing up was a lot of pleasure. Even when I wrote my piece about pressing our hair, I said that that ritual was also a time of bonding, pleasure. We ate. We fried fish on Saturday. And your hair was pressed. And it was fun and it was a joy, and a lot of times I think if we define the nature of our oppression, we can focus too much on how something became a mark of shame.

I mean, if we cannot fully articulate our pain, then we're not allowed to fully articulate our pleasure either. And the film, very loudly declares that there is pleasure to be found in our hair. There is beauty there.

JULIE: And the whole experience—the ritual of dealing with hair grooming—that's pleasurable. The sitting in, everyone remembers sitting in between some other woman's legs, having your hair brushed and braided. The feeling of two knees on your cheek.

BELL: It's not only in relation to questions of black female beauty that the film is unique. It breaks new ground in its portrayal of darker-skinned black people. We have absolutely no cinematic tradition in which the darker-skinned black male or female body is seen as beautiful. And I thought that we were also seeing a different portrait of black men, or black male physicality there. There is none of that traditional focus on violence.

I think, for example, of the contrast between the image of a dark male body like Danny Glover's in the film *Witness* and what you do with these dark, very physical, black male bodies, which are, as we used to say in the old tradition," much man." I mean, clearly, these black men are much man, but you give them qualities of tenderness. And I found that the scene where Eli meets his cousin on the road and they go through that process of physical bonding, there is something very tender there. Can you talk a little bit about that scene?

JULIE: Well, it's a scene where the characters are kind of misreading one another's intentions, and I'm trying to show at the same time these nonverbal methods of communicating that we have created since the time of slavery. It's all about communication and misreading, and understanding and articulating, with a little reminiscence of African martial arts thrown into it.

In this scene, Eli thinks his cousin is teasing him. His cousin is really just asking him seriously about going north. They do all this dialogue in the context of tussling around. This physical thing that men have—I wanted to have a scene that was tension-filled, but kind of loving. Bittersweet.

BELL: It seems to suggest that something else can happen within the framework of male physicality other than violence.

JULIE: Righto.

BELL: And that bonding on the physical plane can be an expression of tenderness. And I think we see that throughout the film.

JULIE: Especially with this character, the cousin. His character in the script is called the Newlywed Man, and he plays against the Newlywed Woman. Theirs is a visual subplot; all you see of them is their making love, embracing one another, caressing whispering sweet nothings.

BELL: His bride is a very Nubian-looking character.

JULIE: Yes, because as a black woman I needed to see a relationship between a black man and a black woman that was not just about lust, was not just about sex or violence or some kind of platonic, mother/grandfather type of situation. I want to see loving relationships. And every time we see the Newlywed Man and his Newlywed Wife, they are expressing their love.

BELL: They are looking into one another's eyes, so there is no sense that this is a subject/object relationship, one subordinate to the other. There is this mutual process of gazing. And I think again—

JULIE: This tenderness.

BELL: —those narratives in the film tend to go unnoticed by many critics and viewers.

JULIE: And he shows that same tenderness, but with a male physicality attached to it when he has that confrontation with Eli on the path.

BELL: And yet there is a quality of gentleness and tenderness in them. And, again, that is not often seen on the screen, either in a movie like *Witness* or in a movie like *Boyz 'n the Hood*.

But let me ask you this question, because this film is so powerful in terms of the images: Do you feel that the images at times threatened to undermine the narrative of the film or overwhelm the audiences?

JULIE: *Daughters of the Dust* is not what "Hollywood" would call a plot-driven story. I think images do tend to overwhelm the story, the plot, because, like I said earlier, we are being privileged to see so many new things, visually. We're learning new things. And we're hearing things said in a new way, in the Geechee dialect.

[55]

There are so many different layers of the new that when some people experience this, as they process it they lose a sense of the plot, the story. All they retain is pretty much the subject and the theme, and the emotion.

BELL: Well, I know that you worked in collaboration with A.J. on this film. Can you speak a little bit about that process of collaboration, because it's so easy for people to look at a film like this, one that focuses on images, and feel that it's solely the camera work that makes the film.

JULIE: Well, I would say it was a collaborative effort between myself, A.J. and Kerry Marshall, the production designer. Together we worked to come up with the tone, the texture, the feel, the sense of place, all of that. We started working on *Daughters* two years before we went down to shoot it, and Kerry was involved at that stage too. The bringing together of so many different images that have never been shared or expressed, and wanting to have all of these images referenced by something that was real, something that had resonance to it, required a lot from each one of us in a collaborative effort.

Kerry brought photographs, drawings, etchings, sketches, whatever he could find, and he'd say, "Is this what you mean? Is this what you mean?" Or sometimes I would try to express things to him about, say, the indigo plantation, and one time I expressed it to him and he didn't really get it. He created something totally different and said, "Is this it?" And I said no, that's not it. And then, finally I was able to find a picture of the huge dome pits of swirling blue indigo they would have in a West African indigo processing plant. And then he went back and created that. And then I would go to A.J. and express to him how I wanted the scene to look in terms of the density of the smoke, the color, the movement of the unborn child. All of this. How the camera was gonna move. So we would sit around, I would come up with the theme. Kerry would come to me with ideas that would often broaden the look of the scene, and then A.J. would come up with different ways of shooting it, of lighting it. And that's how we worked together.

BELL: Well, it's a marvelous collaboration, and it's interesting to think of collaborations and traditions of affinity. When I think of you and other filmmakers, I certainly never think of you with the sorts of filmmakers you're often compared

(above) Snead at work.

*(following spread) Hagaar and Viola at Nana's
goodbye ritual.*

Yellow Mary and a young family member.

(above) Nana surrounded by "daughters."

(following spread) Close-up of Eula and Yellow Mary

Nana cries.

with—Spike Lee, John Singleton. I think of them as a younger generation of film-makers, not in terms of age but in terms of their experience. And when I think of you, I think of traditions like that of Kathleen Collins Prettyman. I think of Charles Burnett. I think of black independent filmmakers who have not always received the kind of attention that a Singleton or a Spike Lee receives.

But there are scenes in Burnett's film *To Sleep with Anger* that clearly suggest scenes in *Daughters of the Dust*. I'm not saying they're derivative, but there is a rela-tionship in the different way of looking that is being created.

JULIE: In fact, Charles Burnett was in town for a film festival screening *To Sleep with Anger* while I was trying to cut forty minutes of *Daughters of the Dust* for a work print. And I grabbed him and I brought him over here, because I've known Charles for many many years and I've worked with him on several films. And I sat him down and I screened all of *Daughters of the Dust* for him and I said, help, help, what can I eliminate to get us down to 113 minutes? And he looked at it and he gave me some very good advice.

He said, "What you're fighting here is trying to make the men's story equal to the women's story." He said, "Go ahead and make it the women's story, because that's whose point of view it is anyway, and stop trying to give equal time to the black men." And at that point I was able to leap on it and say, yeah, I guess that's where it is. There were so many scenes eliminated. We shot so much more than what you see in the finished film.

BELL: I think some of the efforts Tinh T. Minh-ha has made in her films are akin to strategies I see in *Daughters of the Dust* and, hopefully, people will begin to place *Daughters of the Dust* critically in a world not only of black independent film-makers, but also in the larger world of filmmaking. Because to know you as a film-maker is to know someone who has looked at film and studied it from the angle of production as well as theory. So we're not seeing a straight line from one black filmmaker to another, a continuum from Oscar Micheaux to Julie Dash. But we're seeing a Julie Dash who is a world-class filmmaker drawing from several different traditions.

In fact, I think some people have difficulty with *Daughters of the Dust* because they experience it as a "foreign film." Can you say a little bit about that, because it has that aura of difference.

JULIE: Well, I embrace that criticism. I say, great, it is a foreign film because, as I've been saying, it's a film that privileges black women first, then the black community and white women. The feelings that evokes about African Americans are foreign, because what audiences have seen over the years has been very simplistic. Things that appeal to baser instincts. And now we have a film that is both complicated and complete, with a lot of different meanings. And you have to bring some of your own experiences to it to get the full meaning.

BELL: Let me give an example of that. I think of the lesbian relationship between Yellow Mary and Trula, and it's very interesting to me that The Gay and Lesbian Alliance Against Defamation awarded a prize to *Fried Green Tomatoes* for being the best Hollywood film this year that had "lesbian content."

JULIE: But that's the key: this is not a Hollywood film.

BELL: It seems to me that a lot of people would not see "lesbian content" in your film precisely because black filmmaking is often seen as being homophobic or misogynist or sexist. But when Nana Peazant is talking with Yellow Mary, it's clear that Yellow Mary really is a new kind of woman. And it is obvious that her newness doesn't just involve her historical experience of rape and exploitation, but her own sexual choices.

JULIE: I always keep going back and prefacing everything with my research. In my research I found that most prostitutes of that time were involved with other women. Their "significant others" were other women, so they were bisexual. And in developing Yellow Mary's character I realized that she, as an independent businesswoman would not be traveling alone. In fact, she would have a significant other person. But let me backup a bit. I'm trying to be careful, because now the actress is going around saying that she was never supposed to be gay in the film. Early on, when I wrote it with an Asian American woman as Yellow Mary's traveling companion, they were indeed lovers. I took her out of the film and then I reinserted her as a very light-skinned African American woman. And that is how we got the Trula character. But, yes, they were very clearly lovers.

BELL: And I think this comes across to the audience. I think that the film manages, while giving us a lot of concrete information, to maintain its aura of mystery and magic. And it seems to me that it's crucial that the film does not identify them directly as lesbians any more than it identifies them directly as prostitutes.

JULIE: It's the same with the rape.

BELL: Right. We know it through the associations, through the types of things that are being said when Yellow Mary says that she is not somebody who is gonna be working in the kitchen. We know that she disavows a certain kind of domesticity.

JULIE: She becomes just another of the many kinds of African American women who appear in the film, and in the world.

Dialogue between bell hooks and Julie Dash

A Word

FROM GREG TATE

I'VE SEEN *Daughters of the Dust* eleven times, fought back tears at every screening, and lost the fight each time. What makes me weep are not plot points or the travails of individual characters, but those bruising moments that brush up against the black historical tragedy. There's the scene where the great-grandmother recalls how it became the necessity of the slaves themselves to remember every birth, death, marriage, and sale, so as to stave off the possibility of incest between relations. There is the scene where she tells Eli that when he leaves the Sea Islands, he's not "going to no land of milk and honey." As it echoes through the past, *Daughters* echoes around our chilly bones.

Julie Dash's film works on our emotions in ways that have less to do with what happens in the plot than with the ways the characters personalize the broader traumas, triumphs, tragedies and anxieties peculiar to the African American experience. When Yellow Mary speaks of "fixing the titty" so that she can no longer be surrogate mother to her white infant charges, or of being sent home by the employers holding her captive like a slave, we are made to feel not just Yellow

Mary's pain and anger but the psychic scars inflicted on African people since the slave trade began.

Of course, it is in *Daughters'* representations of black women's beauty, particularly dark-skinned black women, that the film breaks cinematic ground. If this aspect of the film seems to scream for attention, it's well that it should after eight decades of omission of dark-skinned sisters in cinema. Check that history and you'd think that compared to white women or their own lighter-skinned sisters, dark-skinned women had no glamour that any camera could see. Or certainly none that could withstand the platinum blonde heat of the bombshells, or the amber fires of the plantation mulatresses, without scurrying for cover in a dowdy, dumpy mammy gown.

Daughters sent all that nonsense screaming and kicking to the curb. Now we all know better, if we didn't know before, and the notion of genetically lightened black femininity as an ideal will have to explain itself.

Those who would limit *Daughters'* achievements to its skin-tone milestones and chromatic correctness, or to the seductive mesmerism of Arthur Jafa's (A.J.) camera work, though, miss the high literary achievement of Dash's script. In it she somehow managed to produce a film about the historical subtext behind black people's surface emotions. Look to the written page, where films are always born but can never be said to have lived, and you'll see this. Read the script and you'll realize that the film's emotional power was embedded in Dash's vision and conception. This is no piddling matter, and the next fool that tries to make like there's no story in *Daughters*, just give 'em a copy of this book.

Nor are the spiritual and psychological dimensions of *Daughters* to be trifled with. The connections Dash makes between the middle passage and African American spiritualism, between rupture and continuity by way of professing faith in ancestral guidance, speak to the familiarity and confidence with which she approaches African American spiritualism.

Praised for its photographic sculpturing, *Daughters* is also a powerful piece of African American psychological modeling and portraiture. Like Toni Morrison's *Beloved*, it is less about the horrors of the slave experience as a way of life than about how that horrific institution shaped the interior lives and life choices of the slaves and their descendants. It is, finally, slavery that transformed African people into American products, enforcing a cultural amnesia that scraped away details without obliterating the core. We remain in a middle passage, living out an identity that is neither African nor American, though we crave for both shores to claim us. It is *Daughters'* achievement to represent this double alienation as an issue for the community as a whole, and as personal and interpersonal issues for the film's principal characters.

The ways in which history and character are interwoven in *Daughters* is painful, poignant, and insightful, especially where the black women who are its central focus are concerned. So that when Yellow Mary advises Eula not to divulge to her husband, Eli, the identity of her rapist for hear he'd be lynched, we know that black women of the period had to check their outrage at violation for fear it would bring more violence and death upon their men. *Daughters* continually disinters the sources of black pain, repression, silence, and denial.

I have never pretended to be non partisan about *Daughters*. I am proud to have known Julie Dash and A.J. through their decade-long march into the theaters. It has been for them, ten years of poverty sweat, parenting, and commitment to the black independent film movement and to the highest intellectual, spiritual and political ideals laid down by their artistic ancestors: Oscar Micheaux, Ida Wells Burnett, Malcom X, Zora Neale Hurston, Ozu, Antonioni, Haile Gerima, Charles Burnett, and Larry Clark.

The idea that black art can be cosmopolitan and Afri-centric bursts from every frame of *Daughters*, as does the idea that the truly Afri-centric is the very essence of cosmopolitan universality. What *Daughters* captures more expansively than any black film since Bill Gunn's *Ganja and Hess* is the range of religious, sexual, and geographical choices available for our nomadic souls.

Marking our ambivalent quest for worldly experience and a sense of ancestral place, *Daughters* displays intellectual rigor and passion for the wandering spirit sons of African American people. Dash refers to the film as a kind of family album. As long as we question the weight of the past that bears on our future, we should study and treasure its pictures and memories with abiding adoration and concentration.

THE SCRIPT:

Daughters of the Dust

FADE IN:

EXT. SHAD PEAZANT'S FIELD, 1860's - DAY (SUNSET)

CLOSE ON

The rough, INDIGO, BLUE-STAINED, hands of an African
American woman, YOUNG NANA PEAZANT. She is wearing
an indigo-colored dress and holding Sea Island soil
within her hands. There is a great WIND blowing.
The soil, like dust, blows from her hands and through
her fingers.

                        CUT TO:

EXT. IBO LANDING, 1902 - DAY (SUNRISE)

A place where barges and small boats from larger
ships can land. A decaying SIGNPOST READS:

                   IBO LANDING

We hear the sound of cicadas rustling the Palmetto
forest.

ANGLE ON - WATER

NANA PEAZANT, now age 88, the great-grandmother of
the Peazant family is rising out of the water. She
is fully dressed. Nana is wearing TWO BELTS, one
around her waist and another belt strapped low around
her hips.

                        WOMAN'S VOICE (O.S.)
                I am the first and the last.
                I am the honored one and the
                scorned.

                        CUT TO:

                              NANA PEAZANT =
                                OBATALA

                            [75]

INT. PEAZANT SHANTY - ELI & EULA'S BEDROOM - DAY

As the camera explores this bedroom, WOMAN'S VOICE
continues,

YELLOW MARY =
YEMAYÁ

"MOTHER OF
THE SEA,
THE MOTHER
OF DREAMS,
THE MOTHER
OF SECRETS"

                    WOMAN'S VOICE (O.S.)
        I am the whore and the holy one.
        I am the wife and the virgin.
        I am the barren one, and many
        are my daughters.

"THUNDER, PERFECT,
MIND"

                              CUT TO:

FROM GNOSTIC
GOSPELS

EXT. DOWN RIVER - DAY

YELLOW MARY PEAZANT, a light-skinned, well-dressed
prostitute is traveling to Ibo Landing on an open
BARGE.

CLOSE ON - YELLOW MARY

She is wearing a HAT with VEILING, beneath the mesh
she wears too much make-up. Around her neck she
wears a ST. CHRISTOPHER'S CHARM. O.S. WOMAN'S VOICE
continues,

ON - YELLOW MARY

                    WOMAN'S VOICE(O.S)
        I am the silence that you can
        not understand. I am the
        utterance of my name.

FADE OUT.

FADE UP ON TITLE: DAUGHTERS OF THE DUST

EXT. ESTABLISHING THE SEA ISLANDS - DAY

YELLOW MARY'S ARRIVAL
UNIVERSAL
RITE OF
TRANSITION

We see an island chain extending along the Atlantic
coast, from Savannah to the north of Charleston. These
islands are separated from the mainland by wide marshes
and tidal estuaries. We HEAR the sound of "talking
drums" relaying messages from island to island, sound
continues over TITLE:

        THE SEA ISLANDS OF THE SOUTH, 1902

                        CUT TO:

TRULA = OSHUN
"THE GOLDEN COQUETTE"

EXT. HILL OVERLOOKING THE SEA - DAY

ANGLE ON - BILAL MUHAMMED

Performing his morning prayer, in what
little of the Arabic he remembers.

                                        DISSOLVE TO:

CLOSE ON

Bilal's homemade KORAN and his hands in prayer.

                                        DISSOLVE TO:

EXT. RIVERBANK - DAY

VIOLA PEAZANT, a Christian missionary, and MR. SNEAD,
a "Philadelphia-looking Negro," are waiting along the
riverbank for transportation. Mr. Snead,
a photographer, has his equipment stacked all around
them. Viola waits patiently, Mr. Snead looks concerned,
they appear to be in the backwoods of nowhere.

ANGLE ON RIVER

A BARGE bearing Yellow Mary and her traveling companion,
TRULA, arrives to pick up Viola and Mr. Snead. Viola
stunned by Yellow Mary's presence on the incoming barge.

                                        CUT TO:

EXT. BARGE - DOWNRIVER - DAY

En-route to Ibo Landing. The barge is overcrowded with
luggage, photography equipment, three boatmen, Viola,
Snead, Yellow Mary and Trula.

CLOSE ON - VIOLA PEAZANT

                        VIOLA
                 (embarrassed, trying to
                  cover her true feelings)
            I can't believe it. I had no
            idea. Cousin Mary. . .
                 (to Mr. Snead)
            Praise the lord, Mr. Snead.

                        (more)

[77]

                          VIOLA (CONT'D)
                    (very formal, indicating
                    Yellow Mary)
                My dear cousin, Mary Peazant.
                This has turned out to be a very
                special day for the Peazant
                family indeed.

ANGLE ON - YELLOW MARY AND TRULA

Lifting her veil, nodding to her cousin.

                          YELLOW MARY
                    (to Viola)
                Viola.

                          MR. SNEAD
                    (to Yellow Mary)
                Pleasure to meet you, Mary
                Peazant.

ANGLE ON - YELLOW MARY AND TRULA

                          YELLOW MARY
                    (to Mr. Snead)
                Yellow. . . They call me "Yellow Mary."

Yellow Mary and Trula are flirting with the
Photographer. And he, already sweating in the hot
sea island air, seems to be wearing thin under
Trula's silent watch and Yellow Mary's studied,
veiled gaze.

ANGLE ON - MR. SNEAD

He is confused, no one has bothered to introduce him
to Trula. To make matters worse, Trula's skin color
is more "Yellow" than Yellow Mary's. Snead looks to
Viola for clarification.

ON - VIOLA

Trapped on this barge with two prostitutes and the
man she is trying to impress, Viola smiles
uncomfortably.

                          VIOLA
                    (about Yellow Mary)
                Our fathers were brothers. . .

                          (more)

                         VIOLA (CONT'D)
                    (nervously)
          Of course, compared to some
          people, Yellow Mary's isn't all
          that light-skinned, but. . .
                    (a few beats, then)
          "Yellow Mary," I'd like you to
          meet my photographer, Mr.
          Snead.

We're not sure whether Yellow Mary wants to fuck him,
or is just fucking-with-him as her eyes linger on the
Philadelphia-Negro, totally ignoring her cousin Viola
and her seemingly endless chatter.

                         VIOLA (CON'T)
                    (to Yellow Mary)
          I've commissioned Mr. Snead to
          document our family's crossing
          over to the mainland.
                    (into Shakespeare now)
          "What's past is prologue. . ."
                    (to photographer)
          I see this day as their first
          steps towards progress, an
          engraved invitation, you might
          say, to the culture, education
          and wealth of the mainland.
                    (to Yellow Mary)
          Yellow Mary...wouldn't you
          agree...?

ANGLE ON - YELLOW MARY AND TRULA

Looking at one another and laughing uncontrollably.

ANGLE ON - VIOLA AND MR. SNEAD

Viola feels like a fool and Mr. Snead is embarrassed
to have witnessed Viola humiliated. It's going to be
a long, hot ride upriver. The tide embraces them,
guiding them homewards, to Ibo Landing.

                         CUT TO:

EXT. IBO LANDING - DAY

Deep within the island's interior, TWO WOMEN, in
rhythmic unison, are husking wild rice with a MORTAR
and PESTLE.

                         [79]

We HEAR sounds of FIELD CRIES coming from black
families who occupy this region. As the O.S. sound
continues, we begin to distingush some of the cries
as. . .

                         FIELD CRIES   *FIELD CRIES = BLUES = JAZZ*
             I...bo..., Fu...la...ni...,
             Da...ham...ee...

These names are half-sung, half-cried. We can sense
a tradition here. A tradition of lost souls calling
out to identify a half-remembered, half-forgotten
"people" they were taken from.

                                        CUT TO:

EXT. PEAZANT SHANTY - DAY

Beyond the sand dunes, the swamps and the brackish
salt pits, we find a SLOPING SHANTY where the
Peazant family lives. The color INDIGO is painted
on the window frames and around the door. FRIZZLED
CHICKENS scratch their way in front of the shanty
looking for conjure bags. We HEAR the O.S. voice of
a young girl, the Unborn Child,

                         UNBORN CHILD (O.S.)
                          (recollecting)
                 My story begins on the eve of my
                 family's migration North. My story
                 begins before I was born. My great
                 great grandmother, Nana Peazant, saw
                 her family coming apart. Her
                 flowers to bloom in a distant
                 frontier.

                                     DISSOLVE TO:

INT. PEAZANT SHANTY - ELI AND EULA'S BEDROOM - DAY

EULA is lying next to her husband ELI PEAZANT.
Eula turns towards him but Eli remains with
his back to her. The O.S. voice of the Unborn
Child continues,

                         UNBORN CHILD (O.S.)
                 And then, there was my ma and
                 daddy's problem. Nana prayed and
                 the old souls guided me into the New
                 World.

ANGLE BENEATH THEIR BED

Eula reaches down beneath the bed to pick up a
TIN CANISTER. We see a GLASS OF WATER that has
been placed on top of an envelope.

To SEND A MESSAGE TO A DECEASED PERSON

CLOSE ON - GLASS OF WATER

If you look closely, you may see your future.

                    CUT TO:

INT. PEAZANT SHANTY - CHILDREN'S ROOM - DAY

MYOWN PEAZANT, 15, is sleeping with her sister
IONA, 17, and their younger cousins.

                    UNBORN CHILD (O.S.)
              I came in time for the big
              celebration, to be among my
              cousins, my aunties and uncles...

                    CUT TO:

INT. PEAZANT SHANTY - LIVING ROOM - DAY

Everything is boxed and packed for moving.
White summer DRESSES are hanging around the
room, "airing out." The walls are papered
with NEWSPAPER that is peeling away from the
wood. PEAZANT MEN and WOMEN are sleeping,
crowded into the front living room.

NEWSPAPERED WALLS TO PROTECT FAMILY FROM EVIL

ANGLE ON - THE NEWLYWEDS

Secretly creeping from the confines of
communal sleeping quarters. In hurried
movements they prepare a pallet on the floor
to make love.

                    UNBORN CHILD (O.S.)
              I can still see their faces,
              smell the oil in the wicker
              lamps. . .

                    CUT TO:

BACK TO - CHILDREN'S ROOM - DAY

Myown is awakened by the SOUNDS coming from
the newlyweds in the front room.

CLOSE ON - MYOWN

As she peels away six or more QUILTS used to
ward off the cold damp night, Myown rises and
finds BLOOD STAINS on the sheet beneath her.

*MUST LOSE SUBPLOT
OF MYOWN'S FIRST
MENSTRUATION
TO SAVE TIME*

                    UNBORN CHILD (O.S.)
          I can still hear the voice of Auntie
          Haagar calling out for her
          daughters, Iona and Myown, and
          teasing the newlyweds.

                                        CUT TO:

BACK TO - FRONT ROOM - DAY

The newlyweds are making love.

                                        CUT TO:

EXT. BARGE - DOWNRIVER - DAY

POV - YELLOW MARY LOOKING THROUGH KALEIDOSCOPE

ECU on twisting, changing, multi-colored
designs. O.S. voice of Mr. Snead, the
Photographer, talking about his
Kaleidoscope.

                         MR. SNEAD (O.S.)
          Kalos. . . Beautiful.

CLOSE ON - MR. SNEAD

                         MR. SNEAD (CONT'D)
          Eidos. . . Form. Skopein. . .

CLOSE ON - YELLOW MARY AND TRULA

Yellow Mary is peering through the
Kaleidoscope, Trula playfullly leans forward,
looking into the front end

                         MR. SNEAD
          If an object is placed between two
          mirrors, inclined at right angles,
          an image is formed in each mirror.

ON - YELLOW MARY AND TRULA

With the Kaleidoscope.

>   MR. SNEAD (O.S.)
>   Then, these mirror images are in
>   turn reflected in the other mirrors,
>   forming the appearance of four
>   symmetrically shaped objects.

ON - MR. SNEAD AND VIOLA

Viola is sucking on hard candy and peering
off into the distance. The boatmen are
watching and listening with a keen interest.

>   MR. SNEAD
>   (very pleased with himself)
>   Oh, I think it's just a wonderful
>   invention. It's beauty, simplicity
>   and science, all rolled into one
>   small tube. I think the children
>   will enjoy it.

ON - VIOLA

Not really listening, she recognizes
something.

>   VIOLA
>   (very excited)
>   Yellow Mary, look!

Viola points

POV - VIOLA

They are passing a small deserted island, we
see the remains of a small crumbling shanty.

>   VIOLA (O.S)
>   Uncle Spikenard lived there.
>   Do you remember him?

ANGLE ON - YELLOW MARY AND TRULA

Still playing with the Kaleidoscope. Yellow
Mary glances at the island, then returns her
attention to the Kaleidoscope.

                         VIOLA (CONT'D)
                    (not waiting for an answer)
               I guess not, I was just a young
               Miss too, then. He was from
               Africa, and just after the war,
               he moved from the plantation to
               that little house on the
               waterfront.

ON - VIOLA AND MR. SNEAD

                         VIOLA
               Remember how when Uncle Spikenard
               used to get angry, he'd talk funny
               so the children couldn't
               understand him? He'd speak in
               African words and sounds.

Viola, seeing that she has piqued the
photograher's curiousity, continues

                         VIOLA (CONT'D)
               You know, Uncle Spikenard told
               me, just before the war they'd
               keep boatloads of fresh Africans
               off on some secret islands around
               here.

                         MR. SNEAD
                    (Mr. Educated, to Viola)
               Viola, our government banned the
               transporting of Africans for
               slavery 50 years before the Civil
               War.

ON - VIOLA

Viola, munching on candy,

                         VIOLA
                    (with a knowing smile towards
                     Yellow Mary)
               Not back off on these islands.
                    (to Mr. Snead)
               Noooo! Just before the war, they
               were still running and hiding
               salt water Africans, pure bred,
               from the Yankees.

Mr. Snead is not convinced.

                         CUT TO:

[84]

EXT. SWAMP - IBO LANDING - DAY

Where the tidal waters slow to a stagnant
green muck. Floating in a swampy estuary is
the broken-off remains of a slave ship's
FIGUREHEAD.

ANGLE ON - FIGUREHEAD

Parasites and vegetation are clinging to what
was once a carved representation of an African
Warrior. The Figurehead rocks in the thick
mire, its rotted wooden flesh dumbfoundly
facing a place called Ibo Landing.

                              CUT TO:

EXT. PEAZANT FAMILY - GRAVEYARD - DAY

Nana Peazant, still wet from her morning bath,
throws rice to the left and to the right
before entering.

ANGLE ON - GRAVES

They are covered with SEASHELLS, BOTTLES,
POTS, PANS, old DISHES and other personal
effects of the deceased. There are some
twisted METAL and BROOMSTICK gravestones.
Nana Peazant kneels before her husband's
grave. We see his TOMBSTONE reading:

        Shad Peazant 1802-1863
        Born into slavery. . .
        Died, Monday a free man,
        his seed to blossom. . .

ANGLE ON - NANA PEAZANT

Listening to the O.S. SOUND of "talking
drums." We see tears welling up in Nana's
eyes. She is an elder struggling with the
past and the present. She winds an old CLOCK
resting near her husband's grave as her day
begins. Nana speaks to her husband's grave,

                          NANA PEAZANT
                      (in Gullah with English
                          subtitles)
                  My life is pretty much over an'
                  theirs is just begining, an'
                  I'm not gonna be around to see
                  what becomes of all these free
                  Negroes. . .

                                        CUT TO:

    EXT. PEAZANT SHANTY - DAY

    Freshly laundered QUILTS hanging out to dry
    are snapping in the wind. Handwoven FISHNETS
    are hanging out to dry, an OLD MAN is
    repairing one of the nets. Another elderly
    PEAZANT MAN sits on the edge of the porch,
    staring north. He's "studying on" the future,
    with his eyes locked in the past.

ELi PEAZANT = OGUN   NANA PEAZANT (O.S.)
"GOD OF IRON"   North, they say. North is what
                          they wake up whispering in their
                          husband's ears. That's the word
                          that wets their lips in the
                          nighttime.

    Nearby, Eli, a blacksmith, is forging and
    shaping hot iron with a HAMMER on an ANVIL.
    Not too far from the front door there is a
    tree covered with glass JARS and BOTTLES.

    ANGLE ON - BOTTLE TREE

    Protecting the Peazant household from evil and
    bad luck. The bottles are of various shapes,
    sizes and colors. Sunlight radiates through
    the bottles, throwing a rainbow of hues across
    the Peazant family shanty.
                                          Y
                                          THE SPENT THEIR
    INT. PEAZANT SHANTY - DAY   *LIVES PIECING TOGETHER*
                                          BITS OF COMFORT
    There is a frenzy of washing, dressing and   *AND COLOR..."*
    general preparation. The women are relating
    to their personal BOXES, BASKETS, or CANISTERS
    which contain "scraps of memores"; inside
    their boxes we find toiletries, secret items,
    and intimate possessions. In a series of
    shots we see:

Teenage GIRLS press their hair with a HOT
KNIFE, and use burnt MATCH STICKS to darken
their lovely eyes. FLOWERS soaking in water,
are used as perfume. STRING and STRAW, used
keep their pierced ears open, are now
replaced with GOLD EARRINGS.

A WOMAN WITH A BABY is having her hair
CORNROWED into sections by the family
HAIRBRAIDER.

PEAZANT MEN map out on a piece of paper the
roads and trails that will lead them North.
The hairbraider borrows the pattern of the
roads and trails being etched out on paper by
the men; she creates a hairstyle that is a map
of their migration north by parting,
sectioning and braiding an elaborate hair
design.

                    NANA PEAZANT (O.S.)
              Now everything they own is all
              boxed up, packed up, and ready
              to head North.

A WOMAN with BLUE-STAINED HANDS ironing a
white dress.

A BABY being dressed.

Peazant teenagers waking.

Girl having her ears cleaned by a grandmother.

A girl having her hair braided.

                    NANA PEAZANT (O.S.)
              But when they come today to kiss
              these old withered-up cheeks
              bye-bye, I'm going to have
              something more than farewell
              waiting on them. Ya see, I've
              been working on a plan.

ANGLE ON - FRONT DOOR

We see a man's HAND pushing a folded LOVE
LETTER beneath the front door.

ANOTHER ANGLE

WOMEN are packing FOOD and basic cooking
utensils to prepare a meal outdoors.

ANGLE ON - IONA PEAZANT

She finds the love letter. She begins to
read,

                    IONA (V.O.)
                (reading with difficulty)
            "Mistress Iona Peazant, Dahtaw
            Island, August 18, 1902. . ."

                                        CUT TO:

"Dahtaw"
Gullah for
"Daughter Island?"

EXT. WOODS - DAY

A BLACK FAMILY, and a Native American man, ST.
JULIAN LAST CHILD, are gathering SPANISH MOSS
from live oak trees. We HEAR the O.S. Iona
reading Love Letter,

CLOSE ON - ST. JULIAN LAST CHILD

Pulling moss from the trees as Iona is reading
what he has written to her.

                    IONA (O.S.)
                    (reading)
            "Iona, with the greatest respect for
            yourself, and the Peazant family, I
            beg that you stay by my side here
            on this island."

INT. PEAZANT SHANTY - CHILDREN'S ROOM - DAY

Iona is pulling things from her secret box
filled with scraps of memories. Among her
things are pieces of Native American jewelry,
made for her by her lover St. Julian Last
Child. Her V.O. reading the love letter
continues,

                    IONA (V.O.)
            "Please do not leave me in this
            flood of migration North."

SCRAPS OF MEMORIES,...
THROUGH THEM WE CAME
TO KNOW OUR MOTHERS,
GRANDMOTHERS, + FAMILY
HISTORY. AND FINALLY
TO KNOW OUR OWN
SELVES..."

BACK TO ST. JULIAN LAST CHILD

Working, thinking about Iona.

                       IONA (O.S.)
         "I feel if I lose you I will lose
         myself. . ."

BACK TO IONA

Iona looks up, almost as if she can see St.
Julian Last Child beside her. Her V.O.
continues

                       CUT TO:

EXT. WOODED AREA LEADING TO THE BEACH - DAY

We see the Peazant Women carrying baskets of
FOOD, POTS, PANS and QUILTS on their heads.
They are walking African style, heads held
high, arms akimbo in a single-file procession.
One woman has a child holding on to her skirt
as they enter upon the sandy beach searching
for a picnic site.

                       IONA (O.S.)
               (reading love letter)
         "Consider the memories that we
         share of growing up together."

EXT. PEAZANT SHANTY - DAY

ANGLE ON WINDOW

Eula Peazant has remained behind, alone, in
the Shanty. She seems troubled. We continue
to HEAR Iona reading O.S. from her love
letter, Iona's words speak to Eli and Eula's
situation.

                       IONA (O.S.)
               (reading love letter)
         "We are the young, the eager up
         from slavery,..."

EXT. CLEARING IN THE WOODS - DAY

Eli Peazant stops to greet St. Julian Last
Child, who is hauling a load of Moss. We
continue to hear Iona reading O.S.,

> IONA (O.S.)
> (reading love letter)
> "Eager to learn a trade, eager to
> make a better life for ourselves
> and our children who will follow."

EXT. BEACH - DAY

In this same bittersweet moment, we come upon
the Newlywed couple, leaning against a tree,
whispering to one another. Iona's O.S. words
express the Newlyweds' innermost thoughts and
actions.

> IONA (O.S.)
> (reading love letter)
> "Our love is a very precious, very
> fragile flowering of our most
> innocent childhood association.
> If fear clouds your decision,
> together we must call out to
> higher forces, that they might
> guide us."

ANGLE ON - ELI PEAZANT

Gesturing, from across the beach, Eli is
trying to communicate with his cousin, the
Newlywed Man, using exaggerated hand signals
and motions. Iona's O.S. reading continues

EXT. PICNIC SITE - BEACH - DAY

When we come back to Iona she is with her
cousins, reading aloud from the love letter

                    IONA (CONT'D)
                  (reading letter)
        "Iona, as I walk towards the
        future, with your heart embracing
        mine, everything seems new,
        everything seems good, everything
        seems possible. Signed, St.
        Julian Last Child.

EXT. TREE - DAY

St. Julian Last Child, the Native American Sea
Island laborer, is seated within a huge oak
tree, "listening" to the O.S. sound of Iona
reading his love letter.

                    IONA (O.S.)
                  (reading love letter)
        "Son of the Cherokee Nation, Son
        of these islands we call Dahtaw,
        Coosa, Edisto, Sapelo, Dafuskie,
        Ossabaw, Kiwa, Wassaw, Paris and
        Santa Helena."

BACK TO - IONA

As her voice trails off to silence, Iona turns
to one of her older cousins. Iona rests her
head on her cousin's shoulder

                    OLDER COUSIN
                  (firmly, to Iona)
        Iona, you'll have to go North
        with us.

Iona sits upright, defiantly,

                    OLDER COUSIN (CONT'D)
        Auntie Haagar won't let you
        stay, we all have to leave.
        We all have to leave together. . .

Huddled together, the young women begin to
silently re-read the love letter.

                    CUT TO:

"DAFUSKIE" = Gullah pronunciation of "THE FIRST KEY" Islands often called "KEYS"

[91]

EXT. PEAZANT GRAVEYARD - DAY

Nana Peazant is cleaning weeds from the family
plot when Eli approaches her from behind. Eli
bends over to place a kiss on her forehead

                        NANA PEAZANT
                    (pretending to be startled)
                Who's that? What're you
                children up to now. . .?

ANGLE ON - ELI

He smiles. Nana pushes him aside,

                        NANA PEAZANT
                    (continuing)
                Get on with you, son, or help me
                clean away these weeds.

ANOTHER ANGLE

Not too far away, some of the teens are
singing and dancing to a ring-and-line game.
A smaller group of youngsters are playing
bubbles with a CORN COBB PIPE.

ANGLE ON MYOWN

She leads them in song and dance.

BACK TO - ELI AND NANA

Nana is seated in front of Shad Peazant's
grave. She is staring off into the distance,
ignoring Eli. She massages her gums with a
CHEW STICK.

                        ELI PEAZANT
                Just because we're crossing
                over to he mainland, it doesn't
                mean that we don't love you. It
                doesn't mean we're not going to
                miss you. And it doesn't mean
                we're not going to come home and
                visit with you soon.

                        NANA PEAZANT
                Eli Peazant, if you don't stop
                grinning at me. . . It's not
                right to tease old folks,
                especially your great-grandmother.

                        (more)

            NANA PEAZANT
You're lucky I've got breath in
me yet. You old goober-head.
        (teasing him)
"Goober Head". We used to call
you "goober head." Remember
that?
        (almost to herself)
Goober means peanut.

Eli digs into his vest pocket.

            ELI
What's this? Something seems
to be stuck in here!

            NANA PEAZANT
        (a serious look, joking)
You know your granddaddy Shad
didn't like to see a woman
chewing tobacco. Ain't that so?
You know that's so.

            ELI
No, Ma'am.

Eli hands Nana tobacco and she cradles it in
her BLUE-STAINED hands.

            NANA PEAZANT
        (serious now, indicating the
        grave)
I visit with old Peazant every
day since the day he died.
It's up to the living to keep
in touch with the dead, Eli.
Man's power doesn't end with
death. We just move on to a new
place, a place where we watch
over our living family. . .

            CUT TO:

BACK TO - MYOWN AND GIRLS ON BEACH

We find Myown is spinning 'round and 'round,
dancing in the center of the ring-and-line
game.

CLOSE ON - MYOWN

While dancing she bends forward, three times
in a downward jerking motion, in sync with
Nana Peazant's O.S. voice.

                    NANA PEAZANT (O.S.)
                    (to Eli)
          Respect your elders! Respect
          your family! Respect your
          ancestors!

                              CUT TO:

BACK TO NANA AND ELI

CLOSE ON - NANA

                    NANA
                    (with compassion)
          You're worried that baby Eula's
          carrying isn't yours. . .,
          because she got forced.

ON - ELI

He tries to stand. He wants to get away, but
Nana Peazant's BLUE-STAINED hands are stong as
she grips his collar.

                    NANA PEAZANT
          Eli, you won't ever have a baby
          that wasn't sent to you.

Eli cannot look directly into her face. To
show respect for his elder, he must turn his
face from hers and listen well. . .,

                    NANA PEAZANT
          The ancestors and the womb. . .
          they're one, they're the same.

                              CUT TO:

BACK TO MYOWN - BEACH

She is being taken into a spiritual
possession. We continue to hear Nana Peazants
words.

                    NANA PEAZANT (O.S.)
          Those in this grave, like those
          who're across the sea, they're
          with us. They're all the same.

                    NANA PEAZANT (CONT'D)
          The ancestors and the womb are one.
          Call on your ancestors, Eli. Let
          them guide you. You need their
          strength. Eli, I need you to make
          the family strong again, like we
          used to be.

                              CUT TO:

BACK TO ANGLE ON - ELI

He pulls away from Nana.

                    ELI
          How can you understand me and the
          way I feel? This happened to my
          wife. My wife! I don't feel like
          she's mine anymore. When I look
          at her, I feel I don't want her
          anymore.

ON - NANA

                    NANA
               (calmly, quietly)
          You can't give back what you
          never owned. Eula never belonged
          to you, she married you.

ON - ELI

                    ELI
               (mocking her)
          Why didn't you protect us, Nana?
          Did someone put the fix on me?
          Was it the conjure? Or bad luck?
          Or were the old souls too deep
          in their graves to give a damn
          about my wife while some stranger
          was riding her?
               (a few beats, then)
          When we were children, we really
          believed you could work the good
          out of evil. We believed in the
          newsprint on the walls. . . Your
          tree of glass jars and bottles. . .
          The rice you carried in your
          pockets. We belived in the
          frizzled-haired chickens. . .

                         (more)

[95]

                    ELI (CONT'D)
The coins, the roots and the
flowers. We believed they would
protect us and every little thing we
owned or loved.
            (in a bare whisper)
I wasn't scared of anything,
because I knew. . ., I knew,
my great-grandmother had it all
in her pocket, or could work it
up.

                    NANA PEAZANT
Eli, never forget who we are,
and how far we've come.

                    ELI
            (shaking his head)
I have to leave here. I don't
have any other choice.

                    NANA PEAZANT
Eli. . . Eli! There's a thought
. . .a recollection. . .something
somebody remembers. We carry
these memories inside of us. Do
you believe that hundreds and
hundreds of Africans brought here
on this other side would forget
everything they once knew? We
don't know where the recollections
come from. Sometimes we dream
them. But we carry these memories
inside of us.

                    ELI
What're we supposed to remember,
Nana? How, at one time, we were
able to protect those we loved?
How, in Africa world, we were
kings and queens and built great
big cities?

                    NANA PEAZANT
Eli,. . . I'm trying to teach
you how to touch your own spirit.
I'm fighting for my life, Eli,
and I'm fighting for yours.
Look in my face! I'm trying to
give you something to take North
with you, along with all your
great big dreams.

                    CUT TO:

BACK TO THE BEACH

Iona and Myown have been taken into a
spiritual possession. We continue to hear
Nana's voice over their actions,

>   NANA PEAZANT (O.S.)
>   (to Eli)
>   Call on those old Africans, Eli.
>   They'll come to you when you
>   least expect them. They'll hug
>   you up quick and soft like the
>   warm sweet wind. Let those old
>   souls come into your heart, Eli.
>   Let them touch you with the hands
>   of time. Let them feed your head
>   with wisdom that ain't from this
>   day and time. Because when you
>   leave this island, Eli Peazant,
>   you ain't going to no land of
>   milk and honey.

>   CUT TO:

BACK TO ELI AND NANA IN THE GRAVEYARD

>   NANA PEAZANT
>   Eli, I'm putting my trust in you
>   to keep the family together up
>   North. That's the challenge
>   facing all you free Negroes.
>   Celebrate our ways.

>   CUT TO:

EXT. PEAZANT SHANTY - DAY

Eli contemplates Nana's words while working at
his anvil. Nana Peazant's Bottle Tree,
perched in front of their house for
protection, seems awfully flimsy. His anger
grows.

ANGLE ON - FRIZZLED CHICKENS

Guarding the front yard.

ANGLE ON - NANA'S CONJURE BAGS

Attached to the house, for protection.

INT. PEAZANT SHANTY - DAY

Everything is boxed and packed for moving.
Eula gathers, to pack, family photos still
attached to the frame of an old tin mirror.
She places these items in a BOX that she
carries. On the window's ledge we see the
remains of HERBS, FRUITS, NUTS and FLOWERS
left to dry in the sun.

                              CUT TO:

EXT. PEAZANT SHANTY - DAY

CLOSE ON - ELI

Eli calmly approaches Nana's Bottle Tree and
shatters it with violent blows.

                              CUT TO:

BACK TO EULA

She is startled and frightened by the SOUND of
breaking glass. Eula turns in exaggerated
SLOW MOTION towards the sound.

                              CUT TO:

BACK TO ELI

He strikes the Bottle Tree again and again.

                              CUT TO:

BACK TO EULA

Cowering in the shadows. Terrified, she
covers her ears to the sound of the
destruction of the family's Bottle Tree.

FADE TO WHITE

FADE IN

INT. EULA PEAZANT'S WOMB

As the Bottle Tree shatters, we HEAR what
sounds like an approaching freight train. We
SEE what appears to be the rush of an oncoming
TORNADO.

CLOSE ON - TORNADO

As this windstorm moves closer, some may
recognize that this twisting mass is actually
a growing EMBRYO - Eula Peazant's UNBORN
CHILD.

OMIT - DUE TO LACK OF FUNDS FOR SPECIAL EFFECTS

                         DISSOLVE TO:

EXT. BEACH - DAY

A great wind is blowing. The Unborn Child is
running along the beach. She appears to be
the age of a five-year-old, she's wearing an
INDIGO-colored BOW in her hair. She's running
towards her parents, Eli and Eula. We HEAR
her VOICE,

                    UNBORN CHILD (V.O.)
          Nana prayed for help. I got
          there just in time.

*THE UNBORN CHILD = "ELEGBA"
(THE ONE WE APPEAL TO OVERCOME INDECISION)*

                         CUT TO:

EXT. BEACH - PICNIC SITE - DAY

CLOSE ON - NANA PEAZANT

A great wind is blowing, Nana turns her face
into the sweet wind and smiles. Nana senses
the presence of the Unborn Child.

                    NANA PEAZANT (V.O.)
          Come, child, come!

ANOTHER ANGLE

The Peazant family is hit by the same sudden
blast of wind and sand. The men and women are
scurrying around after flying objects while
attempting to lay the picnic blankets.

ANGLE ON - MYOWN

Reading an outdated and yellowing TABLOID
newspaper. Myown pauses, to turn her face
into the strong hot wind.

ANOTHER ANGLE - DADDY MAC AND NEWLYWED MAN

Mopping his brow, the Newlywed Man is
quizzically looking up at the sky, Daddy Mac
approaches him from behind and speaks,

                    DADDY MAC
               (to Newlywed Man, about the
               wind)
          He, fresh and sweat. . .like a
          baby's breath.

                              CUT TO:

*MALE AND FEMALE
CHILDREN ARE
ALWAY REFERRED TO
AS "HE" IN
GULLAH
CULTURE*

INT. PEAZANT SHANTY - DAY

From the walls Eula peels off another memento,
a strip of the old newspaper used as
wallpaper. She places these items in her BOX

As Eula turns from the window we find her
husband Eli watching her.

ANGLE ON - ELI

Standing in the doorway to their bedroom, Eli
is covered with sweat, and seething with
anger. He crosses over to Eula, lifting her
as he pins her to the wall.

                    ELI
               (shaking Eula)
          Eula! Tell me, who has done this
          to us. . .?

[100]

Eula is slow to respond, but she instinctively
places a protective hand across her stomach.

                    EULA
          No! Nothing good will ever come
          from knowing. . .

                    ELI
              (grieving for their past)
          Everything good is gone.

Eli, in a moment of tenderness, buries his
head in her chest, Eula tries to comfort him,
and when he lifts his face to her,

OMIT TO
SAVE TIME
                    ELI (CONT'D)
              Our dreams are gone.

Eli bolts from the bedroom.

                                        CUT TO:

EXT. PEAZANT SHANTY - DAY

Eli runs away from the shanty. BILAL,
passing by, tries to greet Eli with
exaggerated hand signals and motions. Eli
does not respond to him.

ANOTHER ANGLE

Eli is nearly trampled upon by a herd of wild
MUSTANGS driving through the woods.

                                        CUT TO:

EXT. WOODS - DAY

The Unborn Child is running through the woods,
we continue to hear the sound of the wild
Mustangs.

                                        CUT TO:

EXT. PEAZANT SHANTY

CLOSE ON - HAAGAR'S FOOT

Raking through the broken GLASS remains of the
Bottle Tree.

A WIDER ANGLE

Reveals the Unborn Child approaching Haagar
from behind. The Unborn Childs pulls on
Haagar's skirt. Haagar studies the Bottle
Tree. A sudden blast of wind and sand moves
Haagar to anger.

CLOSE ON - UNBORN CHILD

She's looking up at Haagar, trying to make
contact with her Auntie.

                              CUT TO:

INT. PEAZANT SHANTY - DAY

Eula hears Haagar outside shouting. Eula
looks out the window, she sees Haagar, but
senses something more. . .

                    HAAGAR (O.S.)
            As God's my witness. . .

                              CUT TO:

EXT. PEAZANT SHANTY - DAY

Haagar, lifts her voice, defying the
ancestors,

                    HAAGAR
            When I leave this place, never
            again will I live in your domain.

                              CUT TO:

EXT. IBO LANDING - DAY

Myown approaches the waters of Ibo Landing,
she drops to the embankment, looking at her
reflection in the water.

A sudden wind blows her hair away from her
face. Myown stares across Ibo Landing as if
she sees something in the water. Her sister,
Iona, runs up behind her,

                    IONA
              (out of breath)
         Oh girl, your're so silly!
              (then, quizzically)
         What are you looking at?

POV MYOWN AND IONA

The barge carrying Yellow Mary, Trula, Viola
and Mr. Snead is pulling into Ibo Landing.

                              CUT TO:

EXT. PICNIC SITE - DAY

ANGLE ON HAAGAR AND NINNYJUGS

NINNYJUGS, Haagar's two-year-old son, is on
her lap fussing, he's trying to open her
blouse so he can nurse. Haagar slaps his
little hands away and continues putting
together a SUGAR TIT, (a wad of honey wrapped
in cloth) to help wean the child from her
breast.

OMIT SCENE-
TO SAVE TIME

CLOSE ON - NINNYJUGS

He takes the sweet "Sugar Tit" from his
mother.

                    HAAGAR
              (to Ninnyjugs)
         Baby, mama's tired, and you're
         getting too old. . .
              (shifting him on her lap)
         And too heavy. Here, take
         mama's "Sugar Tit."
              (kissing his cheek)
         Now scat, little Ninnyjugs!

Sucking on the "Sugar Tit", his urge to be at
his mother's breast is temporarily satisfied.
Ninnyjugs scampers away.

CLOSE ON

Bowl full of a long stemmed green vegetable.
A woman with BLUE-STAINED HANDS is chopping
OKRA.

VIOLA'S MOTHER is cutting up okra for gumbo.
The Peazant children are seated around her.
She playfully puts cut-off okra stumps on
their foreheads. The okra sticks on like
little green horns. Viola's Mother quizzes
the young children,

> VIOLA'S MOTHER
> (to the children)
> Oh, I love you!
> (holding okra)
> Now, this means. . .

> CHILDREN
> (singing out together)
> Gumbo!

She points to a POT

> VIOLA'S MOTHER
> Pot called. . ?

> CHILDREN
> (singing out)
> Sojo.

Testing what she's taught them,

> VIOLA'S MOTHER
> Water. . . Water. . ?

> CHILDREN
> (proudly)
> Deloe!

> VIOLA'S MOTHER
> Fire?

> CHILDREN
> (triumphantly)
> Diffy! Diffy!

> VIOLA'S MOTHER
> (laughing proudly)
> Yes! Now, that's all that
> grandma remembers.

ANGLE ON - NANA PEAZANT

Her BLUE-STAINED hands weaving a basket from dried grass stalks. She looks over at her family preparing a last supper before leaving the island. Nana turns away from them, she turns back to the past. We hear her V.O. thoughts,

> NANA PEAZANT (V.O.)
> I'm the last of the old and the first of the new. The older I get, the closer I get to the ground. This was the worst place to have been born during slavery.

                              CUT TO:

FLASHBACK - EXT. INDIGO PLANTATION - DAY

CLOSE ON

A huge VAT of indigo dye. BLUE-STAINED hands are working the indigo dye through fabric. We continue to HEAR Nana's O.S. voice.

> NANA PEAZANT (O.S.)
> Our hands, scarred blue with the poisonous indigo dye that built up all those plantations from swampland.

END FLASHBACK

                              CUT TO:

EXT. BEACH - PICNIC SITE - DAY

In a series of shots we see the Peazant elders.

ANGLE ON - OLD MEN

Playing an ancient board game called "Wari."

CLOSE ON

The eyes of an old man, golden in color from fever and malaria.

ANGLE ON

Man walking where the waves lap upon the
beach.

ON - VIOLA'S MOTHER

Using a cotton RAG BOOK to teach a TEEN GIRL.

>   NANA PEAZANT (O.S.)
>   Our spirits, numb from the sting
>   of fever from the rice fields.
>   Our backs, bent down forever with
>   the planting and the hoeing of the
>   Sea Island cotton.

CLOSE ON - NANA'S TIN CANISTER

Inside the canister are Nana's scraps of
memories; bits and pieces of Peazant family
memorabilia passed down through the centuries.
Nana removes an AFRICAN LOCK, a piece of her
mother's hair, she studies it closely.

>   NANA PEAZANT (V.O.)
>   I was an elder. And, many years
>   ago, as I lay in my mother's arms, I
>   saw Africa in her face.

ANGLE ON - MYOWN PEAZANT

Lying on the sand, reading a tabloid newspaper
from the mainland.

ON - UNBORN CHILD & PEAZANT CHILDREN

Not too far away we find the Unborn Child
playing with the other children on the beach.
She is looking through a STEREOSCOPE (viewer).

POV - THE UNBORN CHILD WITH STEREOSCOPIC
VIEWER

We see black & white moving pictures of the
overcrowded cities of the North. We HEAR the
voice of the Unborn Child narrating.

>   UNBORN CHILD (V.O.)
>   (recollecting)
>   It was an age of beginnings, a
>   time of promises. The newspaper
>   said it was a time for everyone,
>   the rich and the poor, the
>   powerful and the powerless.

[106]

ANGLE ON - EULA PEAZANT

She arrives late. Eula joins the other women
who are busy preparing the food. She stops in
mid-motion, as if someone has called out her
name. We HEAR Nana Peazant's voice,

EULA = Oya Yansa
"THE spirit of THE
WINDS OF CHANGE"

                         NANA PEAZANT (O.S.)
                    Eula said I was the bridge that
                    they crossed over on. I was the
                    tie between then and now. Between
                    the past and the story that was to
                    come.

Eula smiles and waves back towards Nana
Peazant, who is seated away from the picnic
blankets.

ANGLE ON - NANA PEAZANT

She nods back to Eula.

ANGLE ON - WOMEN PREPARING FOOD

                         CUT TO:

EXT. IBO LANDING BOAT DOCK - DAY

The barge carrying Yellow Mary, Trula, Viola
and Mr. Snead is unloading. One Boatman is
busy looking through Mr. Snead's Kaleidoscope.
Another Boatman is helping Mr. Snead assist
the ladies off the barge, Viola is vying with
Yellow Mary for attention.

                         BOATMAN #1
                    (very excited indeed)
                    This can't be you, Yellow Mary
                    Peazant. You gone nearly ten
                    years, but you look just as
                    young and pretty as the day you
                    were lawfully married.

ON - VIOLA

Teetering on the edge of the barge looking
down at the water,

                         VIOLA
                    (to Mr. Snead)
                    Oooh, the waves are making me dizzy.

As Mr. Snead turns to help Viola, he releases
his grip on Yellow Mary too soon and her open
parasol falls into the water.

CLOSE ON

Boatmen unloading luggage and equipment when
we hear a loud, jolting O.S. FIELD CRY.

ANGLE ON - MR. SNEAD

Almost jumping out of his skin upon hearing
the loud "Eeeee...Yooo....Weeeee.....Up!"
from the island's densely wooded interior.
O.S. sound continues,

                    MR. SNEAD
                 (startled)
          What's, what was that. . ?

                         BOATMAN #1
                    (to Mr. Snead, pointing east)
          Why, someone over there. . .
                    (then pointing west)
          Saying hello to someone over there.

Boatman #2 looks confused, he stops and
listens to the O.S. sound of the field cry,
while Viola presses Yellow Mary to the side.

ANGLE ON - YELLOW MARY AND VIOLA

                    VIOLA
                 (whispering to Yellow Mary)
          Lord, girl, where have you been all
          these years, what happened to you?

Yellow Mary adjusting hat and veiling,

                         YELLOW MARY
                    (a few beats, then)
          Pick a story.

Yellow Mary and Trula chase after Yellow
Mary's parasol floating upriver, leaving
Viola with her mouth open, guessing.

ANGLE ON - BOATMAN #2

Still indignant over the first Boatman's
translation of the field cry.

*SCENE CUT FROM
FINAL EDIT DO TO
LACK OF TIME*

                    BOATMAN #2
                 (to Boatman #1)
        Monday! Monday Capers, now that
        was no, "hello." You know that
        Mr. Manigault telling his brother
        Jacob not to hold lunch for him
        'cause he's still fishing down at
        the cove.

ANGLE ON - BOATMAN #1

Shrugging, slightly embarrassed,

                        BOATMAN #1 (MONDAY
                        CAPERS)
                     (to Boatman #2)
        I'm just try'n to make it plain for
        the stranger. . .
                  (then, to Mr. Snead)
        Ya see, over here we talk this way
        long distance, we don't have to use
        no words.

ON - MR. SNEAD

Feeling awkward and uneasy, he nods
understanding and begins to carefully remove
his "high-tech" photo equipment from the
barge.

ANGLE ON - EQUIPMENT

We see boxes stamped GLASS PLATE NEGATIVES, a
box of FLASH POWDER, a WOODEN TRIPOD is
unloaded and a CAMERA BOX.

                                    CUT TO:

EXT. PICNIC SITE - DAY

Viola's mother sees Viola and Snead arriving
at the beach. She runs to welcome her, and
the rest of the family follows. The family
exchanges greetings with Viola and Snead.

ANGLE ON - VIOLA AND MR. SNEAD

With Bible in hand, Viola pauses to silently
thank Jesus for her safe arrival. She blesses
the family with a wave of her Bible over their
heads.

ANGLE ON - YELLOW MARY AND TRULA

Yellow Mary is shaking her parasol, which
is still wet from the waters of Ibo Landing.
Myown and Iona are with them.

ANGLE ON - PEAZANT FAMILY

Although she's dressed in fine silks, lace and
veiling, the Peazants immediately recognize
Yellow Mary. Simultaneously repulsed by her
and drawn to her, the Peazants stare wide
mouthed as Yellow Mary approaches them.

ANGLE ON

                    HAIRBRAIDER
                (about Yellow Mary)
        That's Gussie's daughter, isn't
        it? Old man Peazant's
        granddaughter has come home! Oh,
        she got ruined, you know. Yellow
        Mary went off and got ruined.
                (then, about Trula)
        And, who is that with her?

                    HAAGAR
                (calling out to her daughter)
        Iona! Go warn Nana Peazant!
                (about Yellow Mary)
        It'll most likely kill Nana to
        see this heifer has returned!

                    IONA
                (weakly protesting)
        But Ma, I don't think.. .

Iona is cut off by the older women pressing in
on Yellow Mary

CLOSE ON - VIOLA

                    VIOLA
                (about Trula's and Yellow
                  Mary's skin color)
        All that yellow, wasted. . .

ON - YELLOW MARY AND TRULA

> YELLOW MARY
> (seeing Eula)
> Is this the same little girl I
> used to rock in Gussie's yard?

Supporting her pregnant belly, Eula runs to
greet Yellow Mary. They rock in each others
arms.

ANGLE ON - HAAGAR AND PEAZANT WOMEN

> PEAZANT WOMAN
> (about Yellow Mary)
> The shameless hussy!

ANGLE ON - YELLOW MARY, TRULA AND EULA

> YELLOW MARY
> (introducing Trula)
> Trula, this is Eula

ANGLE ON - ELI AND THE NEWLYWED COUPLE

The Newlywed Man nudges Eli forward to greet
Yellow Mary; it's a challenge, really.

ON - YELLOW MARY, HAAGAR AND TRULA

Yellow Mary presents Haagar with a gift, a tin
canister of UNEEDA BISCUITS. Haagar takes the
tin of biscuits. She has never seen anything
like this before, she's suspicious.

> HAAGAR
> (holding the biscuits, but
> looking at Trula)
> What is this???

Yellow Mary smiles at Trula

> YELLOW MARY
> (to Haagar, sweetly)
> Store-brought biscuits, Haagar.

Haagar is not about to be outdone.

> HAAGAR
> (eyeing Trula)
> Bread from a store?

She cuts her eyes at Trula.

                    HAAGAR (CONT'D)
          You know, Yellow Mary, they say
          a woman who knows how to cook is
          very pretty.

Myown, overly anxious cuts in

                    MYOWN
                    (to Haagar)
          Ma, can I taste one?

Haagar shoots a look at her daughter, then

                    YELLOW MARY
                    (to Haagar)
          You know I don't like messing
          around in no kitchen. . .

Yellow Mary leads Trula away from the family,
to the beauty and splendor of the ocean before
them. Iona and Myown trail behind them.

ON - PEAZANT WOMEN

                    HAIRBRAIDER
                    (about the biscuits)
          I wouldn't eat them anyhow, if
          she touched them.

                    PEAZANT WOMAN
                    (about Yellow Mary)
          That's right! You never know
          where her hands could have been.
          I can just smell the heifer.

There is a muster of smuggled laughs among the
women.

                    HAAGAR
                    (to the other women)
          The buzzard doesn't circle in
          the air just for fun. . . That
          gal's come back here for something.

FADE TO WHITE

FADE IN ON - ELI

Practicing. Throwing "secret society" hand
signs near the ocean.

ANGLE ON - YOUNG MOTHER, BABY, HAIRBRAIDER

A young girl is nursing a BABY while her
mother combs and braids her hair.

ANGLE ON - NINNYJUGS

Watching and waiting. He looks at the now
empty "Sugar Tit" in his little hands. He has
just been weaned from Haagar's breast. Still,
he remembers.

ANGLE ON - HAIRBRAIDER

Watching Ninnyjugs from the corner of her eye.
She whispers to her daughter, about Ninnyjugs.

                    HAIRBRAIDER
                 (to her daughter)
         Look at 'Jugs waste his time. . .

OMIT SCENE IN FINAL EDIT.

They laugh, she calls out to Ninnyjugs.

                    HAIRBRAIDER
                 (firmly, to Ninnyjugs)
         Get on outta here, Ninnyjugs, go
         on now.

ON - NINNYJUGS

Our hearts go out to him as he walks away with
his bottom lip poked out.

ECU ON - BASKET OF LIVE CRABS

Some crabs are trying to escape, others are
content to wait it out.

ON PEAZANT WOMEN COOKING

Women pluck chickens, chop cabbage, onions and
prepare shrimp for the gumbo. One woman is
poking a knife into a basket of LIVE CRABS.

                         VIOLA'S MOTHER
                     (about the crabs)
                 Girl, what're you doing to those
                 things?

                         PEAZANT WOMAN
                 Just looking to make sure
                 there's no dead crabs in here.
                 Nobody wants to eat a dead
                 crab.

                         VIOLA'S MOTHER
                     (more about the crabs)
                 Why're you making them
                 crawl?

                         PEAZANT WOMAN
                     (to Viola's Mother, annoyed)
                 Girl, you need to be plucking
                 that chicken.

                         VIOLA'S MOTHER
                     (playfully)
                 Throw one of those crabs on
                 Haagar. . .

                         HAAGAR
                     (laughing)
                 Nooo!

The women continue to talk among themselves.
We hear Viola's voice O.S. reading from the
Bible.

ANGLE ON - VIOLA

Viola has cornered several children for a
Bible lesson. Myown is among them, holding
Yellow Mary's open parasol.

                         VIOLA
                     (reading)
                 The earth, O Lord, is swelling
                 with fruitage and reminds us
                 that this is the seed time of
                 life. That not today, and not
                 tomorrow shall come the true
                 reaping of the deeds we do, but
                 in some far-veiled and mighty
                 harvest.

CLOSE ON - CHILDREN

They are afraid to take their gaze from her.
She may have the power to damn them all to
that place called Hell.

> VIOLA (CONT'D)
> (reading)
> Not deceiving ourselves with
> the apparent ease of Eden.
> Looking to that harvest and when
> the earth belongs to the Lord,
> not us, and the fullness thereof.

One little girl blows BUBBLES from a BUBBLE
PIPE.

> VIOLA
> (firmly, to little girl)
> Put that down. Now. . .

ON - VIOLA

> VIOLA
> When I left these islands, I was
> a sinner and I didn't even know
> it. But I left these islands,
> touched that mainland, and fell
> into the arms of the Lord.

ANGLE ON - YELLOW MARY

Where the surf is crashing upon the beach, she
has removed her hat and veil.

ON - MYOWN

Questioning Viola about the mainland.

> MYOWN
> (to Viola, fearfully)
> What's out there, Auntie Viola?

> VIOLA
> (she's inspired)
> Life, child, the beginning of a
> new life.

> MYOWN
> (to Viola)
> Who's out there?

```
ON - VIOLA

                    VIOLA
         Jesus Christ, baby, the Son of God.

                    CUT TO:

ANGLE ON - YELLOW MARY AND NANA PEAZANT

Yellow Mary is sitting at Nana's feet.  Nana
reaches forward to lightly touch Yellow Mary's
lace.

CLOSE ON - NANA PEAZANT


                 NANA PEAZANT
         I heard you were coming.  I've
         been waiting to see you since
         daybreak.

Nana caresses Yellow Mary's hair.

CLOSE ON - YELLOW MARY


                 YELLOW MARY
         I heard the drums too, but I
         didn't know they were talking
         about me, you know. . .

Nana examines Yellow Mary's expensive
earrings.

                 YELLOW MARY (CONT'D)
              (her emotions welling up)
         I wanted to surprise you, Nana.
         That's a hard thing to do in Ibo
         Landing.

Nana touches the ST. CHRISTOPHER'S CHARM on
Yellow Mary's neck.  She cranes her neck
around to examine it more closely.

                 NANA PEAZANT
         No surprises here, Yellow Mary.
              (then)
         What's that you wear around your
         neck?
```

SYNCROTISIM OF RELEGION — THE YORUBA GOD "BACOSO", Founder OF destiny, has been Replaced by ST. Christoper.

[116]

CLOSE ON - YELLOW MARY

                    YELLOW MARY
          St. Christoper's charm, for
          travelers on a journey. . .

                    NANA PEAZANT
               (about St. Christopher)
          What kind of belief is that?
          Does he protect you?

ANGLE ON - MEN'S GROUP AT PICNIC SITE

The Peazant men are "figuring" roads and
trails in the sand when Mr. Snead approaches
them carrying his photography equipment. The
Newlywed Man is assisting Snead.

ON - MR. SNEAD

VISUAL HOMAGE TO   MR. SNEAD
BILL GUNN, DIRECTOR   (about their "figuring" in
OF "GANJA + HESS"   the sand)
                        I see your family sticks to the
                        old ways. . .

Snead's not accustomed to the island's intense
heat and humidity, he removes his jacket as he
attempts to make conversation with the men.

                    DADDY MAC PEAZANT
               (a proud man)
          Yeah, yeah we stick to the old
          ways. But times are changing.
          And you know, Mr. Snead, you have
          to change with the times.

                    MR. SNEAD
               (to an older man)
          Mr. Hail, do you know any of
          those old Africans from your
          plantation days?

                    OLD MAN (MR. HAIL)
          I remember. I remember old
          Cufee. He was an African man,
          a "Salt Water" Negro. He told me
          lots about when he was in Africa.
          He say, they didn't wear no
          clothes over there, just a little
          string around them.
               (adding)
          It was hot over there!

[117]

                           MR. SNEAD
                        (mopping his brow)
                 It's about 110 degrees right here!

The Peazant men, chilling and watching, nod in
agreement.

                                        CUT TO:

EXT. TREE NEAR IBO LANDING - DAY

Myown, Iona and their cousin are throwing
stones in the water at Ibo Landing. Myown is
tying a scarf around her head, like Yellow
Mary's flowing veil. They are watching Yellow
Mary nearby. We HEAR the O.S. sounds of
Yellow Mary and Trula laughing.

A WIDER ANGLE ON

Yellow Mary and Trula are sitting in a tree
laughing loudly and smoking cigarettes. Eula
looks up at them from the ground,
fascinated but confused by their
sophistication.

ON - YELLOW MARY AND TRULA

Passing a cigerette between them and laughing
hysterically. After this we only see
fragments of Trula's body.

CLOSE ON - EULA

                           EULA
                 (cutting into their laughter)
                 As much as I like to fish, I'll
                 never put a pole in that water.

A WIDE ANGLE - YELLOW MARY, TRULA, AND EULA

Eula is pointing out over the water.

                        EULA (CONT'D)
                 That's the spot where the slave
                 girl got drowned by her owner.

```
                    YELLOW MARY
                 (sarcastically)
        Oh, I thought this was Ibo
        Landing. . ?

CLOSE ON - EULA

                    EULA
                 (innocently)
        That doesn't mean you can't
        drown here.
                 (a few beats, then)
        Say again. . .  Say again how
        they say water in Spanish.

ON - YELLOW MARY AND TRULA

                    YELLOW MARY
                 (smiling)
        Agua.

CLOSE ON - EULA

                    EULA
                 (whispering to herself)
        Agua. . . Agua.
                 (then)
        My Ma came to me last night, you
        know.  She took me by the hand.

ON - YELLOW MARY

        Lounging in the curve of the tree.  Yellow
        Mary studies Eula a few beats, then

                    YELLOW MARY
                 (soberly)
        Your titty's been dead
        a long time, Eula.

ON - EULA

                    EULA
                 (explaining)
        I needed to see my Ma.  I needed
        to talk to her.  So I wrote her
        a letter, put it beneath the bed
        with a glass of water, and I
        waited.  I waited, and my Ma
        came to me.  She came to me right
        away.
```

[119]

ON - YELLOW MARY AND TRULA

Yellow Mary sits up, amused by her cousin's superstitions.

                    YELLOW MARY
                (laughing in disbelief)
            Eula! You're a real back-water
            Geechee girl!

Yellow Mary and Trula bust out laughing. Eula is not embarrassed, she stands her ground.

                    YELLOW MARY (CONT'D)
                (about Ibo Landing)
            And this must be the most
            desolate place on the earth,
            and if. . .

                    EULA
                (cutting in, forcefully)
            No, Mary! It's beautiful.

ON - YELLOW MARY

Looking around her, she sees nothing unusual or interesting or beautiful.

                    YELLOW MARY
                ("selling" the place)
            Here it is folks! Ibo Landing,
            reflecting the muddy waters of
            history.

ON - EULA

She looks away,

ON - YELLOW MARY

Gazing lovingly at Eula, she is gripped by her cousin's irresistible charm and provincial beliefs.

                    YELLOW MARY (CONT'D)
                (to Eula)
            Me, myself, personally. . . I
            don't look for my reflection in
            no muddy water, you know.

                    YELLOW MARY (CONT'D)
          The only way for things to happen or
          for people to change is to keep
          moving. People sitting still, men
          sitting still, don't get it with me,
          y'know.
                    (a few beats, then)
          I wish I could find a good man,
          Eula. Somebody I could depend
          on. Not that I'd want to depend
          on him. Just to know that I
          could if I had to.

ON - EULA

Considering what Yellow Mary is saying, she
looks up and smiles, remembering. . .

                              CUT TO:

FLASHBACK - EXT. BEACH - DAY

We see Eula and Eli before her pregnancy, they
are running and laughing along the beach.

END FLASHBACK

                              CUT TO:

BACK TO - YELLOW MARY IN TREE

Powdering her face. We HEAR O.S. of Eula's
voice

                    EULA (O.S.)
                 (to Yellow Mary)
          Mind now, Yellow Mary, you'll be
          itching soon.

                    YELLOW MARY
                 (winking at Eula)
          A little face powder never hurt
          Yellow, y'know. But these blood
          sucking gnats are going to drive
          me back over to the mainland.
          You live like savages back off
          in here.

Yellow Mary throws back her head and screams,
clearing her air space of insects.

> YELLOW MARY
> (very loud)
> Ahhhhhhhhhhhhhhhhhhh. . . . !

Trula laughing, throws a twig at Yellow Mary
trying to make her "hush." Eula smiles to
herself, watching Yellow Mary do her thing and
trying to understand her.

ON - YELLOW MARY

She inhales a gnat and coughs. Then, just as
unceremoniously, Yellow Mary continues to
Eula,

ON - YELLOW MARY

Craning her neck around, back towards the
picnic site,

> YELLOW MARY (CONT'D)
> Y'know, I sure hope they're
> fixing some gumbo. It's been a
> long time since I've had some
> good gumbo.
> (looking up at Trula)
> I had some in Savannah, you know,
> but they didn't put eveything
> in it.

Trula folds her arms across her chest and
looks away,

CLOSE ON - YELLOW MARY

Working Trula's nerves.

> YELLOW MARY (CONT'D)
> I haven't had some good food in
> a long time.

ANGLE ON - MYOWN, IONA AND THEIR COUSIN

Watching the charismatic Yellow Mary and
listening to their private conversation.

                        MYOWN
                  (about Yellow Mary)
            I found her. I found her
            fetching her parasol by Ibo
            Landing.

                        COUSIN
            What kind of woman is she?
            Yellow Mary's no family woman,
            she's a scary kind of woman.

                        MYOWN
                  (boldly, confident)
            She's a new kind of woman.

ANGLE ON - YELLOW MARY, TRULA AND EULA

                        YELLOW MARY
                  (to Eula)
            . . .At the same time, the raping
            of colored women is as common as
            the fish in the sea.

CLOSE ON - YELLOW MARY

                        YELLOW MARY (CONT'D)
                  (pausing)
            You didn't tell Eli who did it,
            did you?

CLOSE ON - EULA

She shakes her head no.

CLOSE ON - YELLOW MARY

                        YELLOW MARY (CONT'D)
            You've got a good man, Eula.
            Somebody you can depend on. He
            doesn't need to know what could
            get him killed.

CLOSE ON - EULA

In silent agony, Eula caresses her swollen
belly. She has been holding so much in for so
many months. Yellow Mary's cautioning words
are comforting, but her words are also a
dismal reminder to Eula of their position in
this Jim Crow society. Eula fears for her
husband, Eli, as well as for the future of her
Unborn Child. And, as we watch Eula, we
continue to HEAR Yellow Mary's O.S. voice.

                         YELLOW MARY (O.S.)
                       (softly, to Eula)
              There's enough uncertainty in
              life without having to sit at
              home wondering which tree your
              husband's hanging from. . .
                       (firmly)
              Don't tell him anything.

A WIDER REVERSE ANGLE REVEALS

The Unborn Child has been with them, near her
mother, Eula, at the base of the huge oak tree
at Ibo Landing. The Unborn Child runs past
them towards the beach. We HEAR the V.O. of
the Unborn Child, recollecting

                         UNBORN CHILD (V.O.)
                       (recalling that day)
              I remember how important the
              children were to the Peazant
              family. . .
                                        CUT TO:

EXT. BEACH - PICNIC SITE - DAY

In a series of shots we see Mr. Snead and the
Peazant men on the beach looking for the
perfect photo setting. Eli is among them, he
is sullen and lags behind the group. We hear
the O.S. voice of the Unborn Child continuing,

                         UNBORN CHILD (O.S.)
                       (continuing)
              . . .And how I had to convince
              my daddy that I was his child.

Mr. Snead sets up his camera and positions the
men.

ANGLE ON - MR. SNEAD

                    MR. SNEAD
              Hold it. . .

ON - PEAZANT MEN

Posing proudly. Daddy Mac speaks to Snead,

>   DADDY MAC
>   If you want to know about those
>   "Africa people," you need to
>   talk to Bilal.

The Peazant men nod in agreement, as the
photographer looks through his lens.

>   MR. SNEAD
>   (whispering to himself,
>   amused)
>   "Salt Water" Negroes. . .

P.O.V. - MR SNEAD THROUGH CAMERA LENS

He sees the Unborn Child in his camera
viewfinder. The Unborn Child is posing next
to her father, Eli.

ANGLE ON - MR. SNEAD

Snead leaps out from under the camera cover.
He looks again at the group of men posing for
him.

P.O.V. - MR. SNEAD

The Unborn Child is not among them.

ANGLE ON - MR. SNEAD

Momentarily stunned, he wipes the sweat from
his brow, perhaps it is the heat and his
imagination.

ON - DADDY MAC

Standing tall, posing.

>   DADDY MAC
>   (continuing to Mr. Snead)
>   They stole Bilal from Africa
>   when he was just a little boy.
>   He came over on the very last
>   slave ship. Bilal came over on
>   "The Wanderer."

>   CUT TO:

EXT. IBO LANDING - TREE - DAY

CLOSE ON - YELLOW MARY

> YELLOW MARY
> (a painfull memory)
> My baby was born dead, and my
> breast were full of milk. We
> needed money, so I hired out to
> a wealthy family. . .some big,
> supposed to be, "muckety-mucks",
> off Edisto Island. High-falutin
> buckra.

She flinches as she recalls. . .

> CUT TO:

FLASHBACK - INT. CUBAN BEDROOM - DAY

We see Yellow Mary nursing a BABY. The baby's
FATHER stands behind Yellow Mary, caressing,
and fondling her other breast. O.S. sound of
Yellow Mary's voice continues to Eula, with
sound of SANTERIA DRUMS.

*CUBAN
SCENES OMITTED*

> YELLOW MARY (O.S.)
> When they went to Cuba, I went
> with them. I nursed their baby,
> and took care of the other
> children.
> (whispering)
> That's how I got "ruint". . .
> I wanted to go home and they
> keep me. . .they keep me.

> CUT TO:

INT. CUBAN BEDROOM - NIGHT

Later, we find Yellow Mary using a folk remedy
to dry up her breast milk. She holds a glass
jar to her breast, inside the jar are smoking
bits of burning newspaper. O.S. sound of
Yellow Mary's voice continues,

> YELLOW MARY (O.S.)
> So I "fix" the titty. . .they
> send me home.

END FLASHBACK

> CUT TO:

EXT. DEVASTATED BEACH - DAY

Not far from the family's picnic site we find
Yellow Mary walking with Trula along a section
of the beach laden with petrified and fallen
trees. Eula follows behind them.

ANOTHER ANGLE

Trula finds an old rotting UMBRELLA that has
been washed ashore. The three women gather
beneath the safety and sanctity of the
seaborne canopy.

ANGLE ON - ST. JULIAN LAST CHILD

Walking along the beach,

ANGLE ON - IONA PEAZANT

Waiting for St. Julian Last Child. She runs
to meet him, they embrace.

                                        CUT TO:

EXT. PICNIC SITE - DAY

Haagar is calling out for her daughter, Iona.

ON - HAAGAR

Who is overseeing the preparation of the food.

                         HAAGAR
                      (calling out)
                Iona! I...on...a! Where's
                that girl?

Lifting a hot pot off of the fire with her skirt,
Haagar starts in on Nana Peazant,

CLOSE ON - NANA PEAZANT

Searching among her can filled with her scraps of
memories.

CLOSE ON - NANA'S TIN CANISTER

Nana removes a small hand-sewn leather pouch. It's
similar to the conjure bags that we saw attached to
the family home.

                        HAAGAR (O.S.)
                    (to Hairbraider)
            I don't see why Nana Peazant
            won't come sit herself down,
            over here, where we can watch
            over her...snakes back off in
            that high grass.

Hairbraider smiles knowingly at Haagar.

                        HAIRBRAIDER
                    (head tilted left)
            Old people think they have all
            the answers.
                    (laughing out loud)
            Carrying around that tin can...I
            don't ever think I saw her
            without it.

Haagar, holding up Yellow Mary's tin can of UNEEDA
Biscuits

                        HAAGAR
            We ought to save this can for
            Eula, She's about as crazy as
            Nana Peazant.
                    (then)
            Sometimes, I think that old
            woman is not in her right mind.

Haagar and the Hairbraider laugh loudly. The other
Peazant women are uneasy, they feel Haagar is being
disrespectful to an elder.

                        VIOLA
                    (to Haagar)
            Haagar Peazant,...that's an old
            woman you're laughing at. Just
            like Eula, you married into this
            family, but she's our
            grandmother. There is nothing
            wrong or harmful in that tin
            can she carries, just some
            old...

                        HAAGAR &
                        HAIRBRAIDER
                    (interrupting in unison,
                    they've heard this
                    before)
            "Scraps of memories..."

Again, Haagar and Hairbraider laugh out loud at their speaking together.

VIOLA
(a true Christian)
Now, I'll be the first to admit that Nana is carrying a lot of old luggage,...she needs to put her soul in the hands of the Lord, but she has built her life around this famly. She's old and she's frightened. What she know of the world outside? Nothing.
Nana was never educated, all she knows are simple things, things that people told her a long time ago.

HAIRBRAIDER
(defensively)
That's why I say Nana Peazant needs to pack her belongings just like the rest of us, and came along. She don't need to stay here like she's somebody with no people.

HAAGAR
(getting evil)
I might not have been born into this family, but I'm here now. And I say, let Nana Peazant stay behind. That's what she wants. We're moving into a new day, she's too much a part of the past.

The women react, even the Hairbraider,

HAIRBRAIDER
Don't let Daddy Mac hear your mouth!

HAAGAR
(determined)
I'm a fully grown woman, and I don't have to mind what I say... I done born five children into the world and put two in the grave alongside their Daddy.

VIOLA ATTEMPTS TO ESCAPE HER HISTORY + THE TRAUMA OF HER SECOND-CLASS CITIZENSHIP WITHIN HER NEWFOUND RELIGIOUS BELIEFS

[129]

                    HAAGAR (CONT'D.
          I worked all my life and ain't
          got nothing to show for it, and
          if I can't say what's on my
          mind, then damn everybody to
          hell!

Viola is stunned by Haagar's anger and frightened by
her harsh words

                    VIOLA
               (to Haagar)
          Mind, now. . ., the Lord is
          listening!

                    HAAGAR
               (indicating Nana Peazant)
          I'm an educated person...and I'm
          tired of Nana's old stories.
          Watching her make those root
          potions... and that Hoodoo she
          talks about.
               (pausing)
          Washing up in the river with her
          clothes on, just like those old
          "Salt Water" folks used to do.
          My children ain't gonna be like
          those old Africans fresh off the
          boat. My God, I still remember
          them. . .

                    HAIRBRAIDER
               (adding)
          And look at that old crazy
          Bilal!

Viola grabs a hold of her Bible, for protection.

                    VIOLA
               (quickly)
          Bilal Muhammed is a heathen. . .

A few beats, then

                    WOMAN WITH BABY
               (in a bare whisper)
          But, he does strange things,
          just like Nana.

                    VIOLA
               (defensively)
          Hush! She's our grandmother!

                    HAAGAR
               (closing in)
          Those old people, they pray to
          the sun, they pray to the
          moon,...sometimes just to a big
          star! They ain't got no
          religion in them. No! This is
          a new world we're moving into,
          and I want my daughters to grow
          up to be decent "somebodies"...
               (a few beats, then)
          I don't even want my girls to
          have to hear about all that
          mess. I'll lock horns against
          anybody, anything that trys to
          hold me back. Now I say, if
          Nana Peazant wants to live and
          die in Ibo Landing, then God
          Bless her old soul.

                    VIOLA'S MOTHER
               (looking up at the sky)
          I think it's going to rain.

                                        CUT TO:

EXT. BEACH

ANGLE ON PEAZANT MEN

Studying their horizon, watching storm clouds
approaching.

                    UNBORN CHILD (O.S.)
          My time was running out. The
          women were arguing and fighting.
          I can still see the fear and the
          hope in the eyes of our fathers.
          They were the sons of drums,
          who could only speak of their
          future. Everyone was just as
          scared as Nana Peazant.

In a series of shots we see the Peazant family
at the picnic site, in the eye of the
storm.

Eli is teaching a teenage boy his "secret
society" hand signals.

Viola is teaching the young women etiquette.

Some of the Peazant men are playing an African
board game.

The Newlywed Woman is getting her hair
braided.

The Newlywed Man walks down a path, and is
ambushed by his cousin, Eli, who wrestles him
to the ground.

          NEWLYWED MAN
    Solomon's in town. Got a colored
    lady with him. Says she's a
    newspaper woman.

In a mock fight, they use secret hand signals
and gestures.

          ELI
     (escaping his cousin's grip)
    Cousin!

RECOLLECTIONS OF AN AFRICAN FORM OF MARTIAL ART

          NEWLYWED MAN
     (smiling)
    We're working on the anti-lynching
    law again. Maybe you want to be
    with us.

          ELI
     (dusting himself off)
    Maybe...But I'm still leaving
    with the rest come morning.

          NEWLYWED MAN
     (innocently)
    Maybe when you go north, you'll
    take with you more than Eula and
    your dreams.

Eli's response takes his cousin by surprise.

          ELI
     (defensively)
    I ain't got no more dreams,
    cousin.

Eli takes one more shot at his cousin, hitting
below the belt.

                    NEWLYWED MAN
              (caught off guard, in pain)
        Aughh! You've been practicing!

Eli storms down the path and enters the woods.
He senses something, not knowing it is his
daughter, and follows her into the graveyard.

                    UNBORN CHILD (O.S)
                  (remembering)
            In this quiet place, years ago,
            my family knelt down and caught
            a glimpse of the eternal.

                            CUT TO:

FLASHBACK - EXT. INDIGO PLANTATION - DAY

Some EARLY PEAZANT FAMILY members are
processing the indigo dyestuff.

                        UNBORN CHILD (O.S)
                      (recollecting)
                  We left our markers in the
                  soil,...in memory of the families
                  who once lived here.

ANGLE ON - UNBORN CHILD

Watching and playing in one of the vats of
indigo dye.

                        UNBORN CHILD (V.O.)
                  We were the children of those who
                  chose to survive.
                      (a few beats, then)
                  Years later, my ma told me she
                  knew I had been sent forward by
                  the old souls.

ECU OF BLUE-STAINED HANDS - MONTAGE:

Wringing out excess blue dye from STEAMING
FABRIC.

Using PADDLES, to beat the fermenting indigo
solution.

Scraping indigo paste, by hand, from the
bottom of the fermenting vats.

Draining, by hand, the residue indigo paste
into bags.

Pressing, and cutting indigo paste into cubes
to be dried in the sun. SHAD PEAZANT, Nana's
husband, is counting the cubes in his own
language. His young son is watching,
listening and learning. We hear,...

                  SHAD PEAZANT
          Eeena!..., Meena!..., Myna!...

END FLASHBACK

                            CUT TO:

EXT. BEACH - PICNIC SITE - DAY

The sun is shining brightly, the storm has
passed them. On the beach the great-great
-grandchildren of Shad Peazant are using the
same counting system with a mailorder Sears
Roebuck catalogue. A "wish book."

                  MYOWN
          (pointing into the book)
        That's mine. That's me, no this,
        that one's you.

The Unborn Child joins them, and with an
indigo stained finger she points to a picture
of a stuffed toy bear.

                UNBORN CHILD (V.O)
        I was traveling on a spiritual
        mission, but sometimes I would
        get distracted.

ANGLE ON - CHILDREN AND TRULA

                  TRULA
          (pointing at catalogue)
        I wish I had this doll...I wish
        I had this doll...I wish I had
        this bed to go inside my house.

                  MYOWN
          (playfully, to Trula)
        You don't have a house!

                    TRULA
              (like a little girl)
    I wish I did. If I did, I'd put
    this bed inside my house. Then
    I wish I had a rabbit.

                    MYOWN
              (to her little brother)
    What'd you wish for, Ninnyjugs?

                    NINNYJUGS
    Everything!

ANGLE ON - HAAGAR

Towering over the children.

                    HAAGAR
              (to her son, Ninnyjugs)
    Ninnyjugs! You can't have
    everything. You've got to go
    like this. Eenie, meenie,
    miney, moe... Catch a piggie by
    his toe. My mother said to pick
    this one right over here. Wish
    for the one right where my finger
    stopped. Now, put that "wish book"
    away. It's time to eat.

ANGLE ON - PEAZANT MEN

They are on a sand dune discussing their
future. Mr. Snead moves some of his photo
equipment to his "darkroom" tent.

                    PEAZANT MAN
              (to the other men)
    I hear they've opened up the old
    Seminole Creeklands for the white
    homesteader.

ANGLE ON MR. SNEAD

                    DADDY MAC (O.S)
    The only thing left for us will
    be scrap iron stills and tenant
    farming... Listen to what I tell
    you... If Roosevelt does
    anything at all, it's going to
    be for Northern industry and not
    for us.

Viola joins Mr. Snead.

                        VIOLA
                   (to Snead)
              Supper's ready, Mr. Snead. We
              will be taking our places right
              up there.
                   (pointing to the picnic site)

While gathering his equipment.

                        MR. SNEAD
                   (to Viola, skeptically)
              "Wish books...", "Salt Water
              Negroes..", Gold earrings, to
              sharpen your vision?

He chuckles to himself. Then, Viola, not
really meaning what she says.

                        VIOLA
                   (slightly embarrassed)
              Oh, they spoil their children
              with dreams, wishes, magic...
              But then, they're the most
              important members of the family.
              The children, and the old souls.

Viola takes Mr. Snead's arm and leads him to
the picnic site.

ANOTHER ANGLE

In the distance we see Yellow Mary and Eula
returning to the picnic site from Ibo Landing.

ANGLE ON - VIOLA

                        VIOLA
                   (watching Yellow Mary)
              Lord, look how she's walking. . .

ON - HAAGAR

                        HAAGAR
                   (about Yellow Mary)
              Is she walking or riding. . ?

SCENE CUT TO
SAVE TIME
IN FINAL EDIT

The woman with a baby joins Viola and Haagar,
adding,

                    WOMAN WITH BABY
                 (about Yellow Mary)
         I think I'm scared of her. . .

                    HAAGAR
                   (to Eula)
         Gather up those kids from Ibo
         Landing. Bring them over here!

                    EULA
                 (to Yellow Mary)
         Let's go and get them. Come
         now!,

Yellow Mary smiles and shakes her head no.
Eula turns back towards Ibo Landing. Yellow
Mary walks past Haagar's gaze...

                    HAAGAR
         Hey! Yellow Mary.
                 (pausing, then)
         They say you're a rich woman.

                              CUT TO:

EXT. PATH LEADING TO IBO LANDING - DAY

Eula searches for the children, who are hiding
from her. She's distracted by the presence of
the Unborn Child and follow her instincts, to
the graveyard.

                         UNBORN CHILD (O.S.)
                   (remembering)
         My Ma said she could feel me by
         her side.

ANGLE ON NANA
                         UNBORN CHILD (O.S.)
         I remember the call of my
         great-great-grandmother. I
         remember the journey home.

ANGLE ON GRAVEYARD

           UNBORN CHILD (O.S.)
    I remember the long walk to the
    graveyard... to the house I
    would be born in...

ANGLE ON - PICNIC SITE

           UNBORN CHILD (O.S.)
    To the picnic site. I remember,
    and I recall.

The family assembles at the picnic site.
Viola is helping Mr. Snead find a place around
the picnic blankets. Having long ago
distanced herself from her people's
"primitive" naming habits, Viola, as an
interesting footnote to Mr. Snead's Sea Island
education, is pointing out some of the
children who have "peculiar" names.

           VIOLA (O.S.)
        (to Mr. Snead)
    It's fifty years since slavery,
    Mr. Snead, but here, we still
    give our children names like
    "My Own" (Myown), "I Own Her"
    (Iona), "You Need Her" (Unita),
    "I Adore Her" (Iadora), "You
    Adore Her" (Euadora)...we even
    have a Pete and Re-Pete...
        (a few beats, then)
    Sometimes these Islanders name
    their babies the day of the
    week or the season in which they
    were born. Not to mention
    everybody has several nick-names.
    Goober, Boy Rat, Hail, Harvest,
    Winter, Pigden, Hardtime. . .

                  CUT TO:

EXT. GRAVEYARD - DAY

Eli's Unborn Child has led him to their family
graveyard, now Eli is walking among the twisted
metal and broomstick GRAVEMARKERS. O.S. we can
still HEAR Viola recounting and recalling the
names of their relatives. Viola evokes the
spirit of their ancestors.

                        VIOLA (O.S.)
            Fantee, Cudah, Ocra, Yono, Cish,
            Alexmine, Jackiemine, Jaspemine,
            Cornhouse, Binah, Shango,
            Obatala, Oya-yansa, Yemonja,
            Eshu Elegba...

ANGLE ON - EULA

Watching Eli in the graveyard.

ANGLE ON - ELI

Kneeling in front of his mother's grave, Eli's
head is turned to the left in frozen reverence
of the spirit that has embraced his body. As
rider would take and mount a wild horse, the
spirit takes Eli, and at the same time,

ESTABLISHING A WIDE ANGLE ON - THE UNBORN
CHILD AND EULA

As the Unborn Child nears Eula, NORMAL MOTION
IS ALTERED. The Unborn Child's spirit enters
the billowing folds of Eula's voluminious
skirt and fades back into her mother. Eula
throws back her head and unleashes a verbal
"ululation" (a call done with the
tongue) that stirs the soul and stills the
waters of Ibo Landing.

                                   CUT TO:

BACK TO PICNIC SITE - DAY

A teen riding a bicycle on the beach with
young Ninnyjugs peddles towards the picnic
site.

ANGLE ON - DADDY MAC

Nana Peazant is seated next to her eldest
son, Daddy Mac, who leads the family in
prayer,

                        DADDY MAC
                    (to the family)
            We're here today to show our
            respect to our family elders,
            and to celebrate our family's
            crossing to the mainland.

                              DADDY MAC (CONT'D)
                    But we're also here today to honor
                    the old souls. Many, who from
                    the very, very beginning of our
                    creation, guided us from one
                    world to another. We're here
                    today, because our parents took
                    us by the hand and taught us to
                    swim the currents surrounding
                    these islands. And they taught
                    us to....
                         (his voice fades)

Nana Peazant is not really listening to her
son's prayer, Nana's recollections go back
much further. . .

                              NANA PEAZANT (V.O.)
                    I recollect how we lived in the
                    time before freedom came, in the
                    old days...

                              CUT TO:

FLASHBACK - EXT. SLAVE QUARTERS - DAY

Bodies in motion. A very awkward version of a
square dance is being performed by some of the
earliest Peazant family members. Some still
have TRIBAL MARKINGS on their faces. This
dance is not a celebration. Their dance is
symbolic of the "new ways" forced upon the
African captives.

ANOTHER ANGLE

Men and Women are exchanging hands and
partners...do-si-doing, picking up
babies and passing them to others.

                              NANA PEAZANT (O.S.)
                         (recollecting)
                    They didn't keep good records of
                    our births, our deaths, or the
                    selling of the slaves back then.
                    A male child might be taken from
                    his mother and sold at birth.
                    Then, years later, this same
                    person might have to mate with
                    his own mother or sister, if
                    they were brought back together
                    again.

EXT. IBO LANDING - DAY

ON EULA

Eula, with her back to the graveyard, is
standing at the bank of Ibo Landing,
telling the story of the Ibo to her unborn
child.

>   EULA (V.O.)
>   (to her unborn child)
>   It was here they brought them.
>   They took the Ibo off the boats,
>   right here where we stand.
>   Nobody remembers how many of
>   them it was, but there were a
>   good few, according to my
>   great-grandmother. She was a little
>   girl at the time.
>   (continues)
>   The ship had just come from the
>   deep water. It was a great big
>   old ship with sails. The
>   minute those Ibo were brought
>   ashore, they just stopped, and
>   took a look around...not saying
>   a word, just studying the place
>   real good. And they saw things
>   that day that you and I don't
>   have the power to see. Well,
>   they saw just about everything
>   that was to happen around here
>   ...The slavery time, the war my
>   grandmother always talks about...
>   Those Ibo didn't miss a thing.
>   They even saw you and I standing
>   here talking.

ANGLE ON - ELI

He has come from the graveyard and he is
walking on the water. Eli is
walking towards the floating, rotting,
Figurehead broken off years ago from the
prow of a slave ship.

>   EULA (CONT'D)
>   When those Ibo got through sizing
>   up the place real good and seeing
>   what was to come, my grandmother
>   said they turned, all of them,
>   and walked back in the water.

Paule Marshall's
from
Praisesong For The Widow

[141]

                              EULA (CONT'D)
                    Every last man, woman and child.
                    Now you wouldn't think they'd get
                    very far seeing as it was water
                    they were walking on. They had
                    all that iron upon them. Upon
                    their ankles and their wrists,
                    and fastened around their necks
                    like dog collars. But chains
                    didn't stop those Ibo. They
                    just kept walking, like the
                    water was solid ground. And
                    when they got to where the ship
                    was, they didn't so much as give
                    it a look. They just walked
                    right past it, because they were
                    going home.

          Eli comes from the water soaking wet. A
          vision has sought and claimed him. Under the
          whip and guidance of his ancestral
          spirit-rider, Eli has witnessed and performed
          things that he could not have done "unridden."

          ON - ELI

          Kneeling before Eula and embracing the
          fullness of her belly. Eli has seen that the
          fury growing inside of Eula's womb is, in
          fact, his Unborn Child.

                                        CUT TO:

          BACK AT THE PICNIC SITE

                              DADDY MAC
                            (to the family)
                    I'm especially proud today to
                    bless the coming child of our
                    Eli and Eula Peazant. Our first
                    child that's going to be born up
                    North. Our child of the future.

          When everyone looks around they notice for the
          first time that Eli and Eula are not present
          at this blessing.

                    HAAGAR
              (not willing to wait)
        Just counting stumps don't clear
        the field. Let's eat.

The silence is broken by laughter and
applause, and the passing and serving of the
food begins. There are OYSTERS steamed in
croaker sacks over open barbecue pits; RICE;
CORN; MELONS; CRAB; SHRIMP; VEGETABLES and
FRUITS.

SOME TIME LATER:

We find them resting. We focus on their eyes
and facial expressions, it is a time of
conversion, of rebirthing to journey North.
The only movement in the frame is that of
Haagar fanning herself and Ninnyjugs.

                              CUT TO :

EXT. BEACH - BENEATH CHINESE UMBRELLA

ANGLE ON - YELLOW MARY AND EULA

                  YELLOW MARY
                   (to Eula)
        Once, I saw a pink satin case
        for jewelry, for rich women, in
        a store window. And it had a
        thing on the side and you turned
        it and music came out. I
        couldn't afford that case for
        myself, and I didn't ask anybody
        to buy it for me. But in my mind,
        I put all those bad memories
        in that case and I locked them
        there. So I could take them out,
        look at them when I'd feel like
        it, and figure it out, you know.
        But I didn't want them inside of
        me. I don't let nothing in that
        case or nobody outside that case
        tell me who I am or how I should
        feel about me.

                              CUT TO:

EXT. ROAD LEADING TO IBO LANDING - DAY

At the same time a procession of Gullah MEN,
WOMEN and CHILDREN wearing WHITE ROBES are
following a BAPTIST MINISTER to their
baptismal waters. They pass by a very old
man, BILAL, age 55, who is carrying a PRAYER
RUG beneath his arm. Bilal is walking in the
opposite direction.

ON - MINISTER

> BAPTIST MINISTER
> (calling to Bilal)
> Bilal! Bilal Muhammed. Come
> join us. Come wash away your
> sins in the blood of the lamb
> Jesus.

> PROCESSIONAL MAN
> (to Minister)
> Let him go, Deacon. Bilal's a
> "Salt Water" Negro. He has no
> shame! He's the master of the
> sun, and the moon.

> CUT TO:

EXT. BEACH - BENEATH CHINESE UMBRELLA - DAY

Trula has joined Yellow Mary and Eula beneath
the umbrella.

> YELLOW MARY
> (to Eula)
> When I leave here...I'll be
> heading up for Canada. Nova
> Scotia. I like the sound of
> that place,...Nova Scotia.

> EULA
> (trying)
> No-va Scotcha.

> TRULA
> (smiling)
> No-va Scotia.

                         YELLOW MARY
                      (to Eula and Trula)
                I never had too much trouble
                making a dollar. Never needed
                nobody to help me to do that.
                I can't stand still. Got to keep
                moving. New faces, new places...
                Nova Scotia will be good to me.

                                          CUT TO:

IBO LANDING - BAPTISM - DAY

ANGLE ON - WOMAN BEING BAPTISED

She is being pulled down into the water by
Baptist Minister and his assistants.

                                          CUT TO:

EXT. PICNIC SITE - DAY

The Peazant women are presenting Eli and Eula
with a wicker BABY BASSINET that has been
passed down through the family for years. The
bottom of the bassinet reads: "Viola Peazant,
born 1867, second year of freedom."

ANGLE ON - VIOLA

Trying to hold back the tears.

ANGLE ON - YELLOW MARY

The children are playing in the wide folds of
 her expensive skirt.

We see Trula walking alone, watching Yellow
Mary's playful actions with the children.

ANGLE ON - EULA

The children are listening to the unborn child
who's moving around inside of Eula's womb.

ANGLE ON - MR SNEAD

Mr. Snead is taking pictures of a group of
children sitting beneath the torn CHINESE
UMBRELLA.

Teenage BOYS and GIRLS are posing for the
Photographer, whose tripod is sinking in
swampy waters. His work is inspired, he's
going for angles and camera positions unlike
the traditional compositions of his day.

                    MR. SNEAD
                (to teens, posing)
          Come closer together...closer.

                    TEEN GIRL
                (teasing Mr. Snead)
          Mind now, Mr. Snead...there's
          'gators back off in these waters.

Mr. Snead quickly goose-steps out of the
water, the teens scream with laughter.

                                    DISSOLVE TO:

On the eve of their departure from the island, we
find Bilal Muhammed giving final instructions to
some of the Peazant boys. He's teaching them how
to perform their Muslim prayers.

                                    DISSOLVE TO:

Mr. Snead the photographer has become
emotionally involved with the family and his
historical documentation of this special day.
With Viola at his side, he is taking a portrait
of her mother.

CLOSE ON - VIOLA'S MOTHER

Posing for Mr. Snead, near the marsh.

                    VIOLA'S MOTHER
                (to Mr. Snead and Viola)
          I don't think about those old
          days much, lately. But when I
          start to study on them, lots of
          things come back to me.

ANGLE ON - OLD SOULS

These slave-community elders are seated facing
the dancers in silent study.

> NANA PEAZANT
> (continuing)
> So it was important for the
> slave himself to keep the family
> ties. Just like the African Griot,
> who would hold these records in
> his head, the old souls in each
> family could recollect all the
> births, deaths, marriages and
> sales.

END FLASHBACK

                              CUT TO:

BACK TO PICNIC SITE

ON - NANA AND PEAZANT FAMILY

Ninnyjugs and a teen boy arrive late on the
bicycle, Ninnyjugs is carrying a small TURTLE.

> NANA PEAZANT (V.O.)
> Those 18th-century Africans...
> the watchers...the keepers...
> the ancestors.

ANGLE ON - DADDY MAC

Holding the turtle. The young boys have
painted an African symbol on the back of the
turtle. An encoded message, an "S.O.S." to
relatives across the sea, markings passed down
through generations who have long since
forgotten their exact meaning.

> DADDAY MAC
> We Peazants, come from a long,
> long line of creation and hope
> begun by those first-captured
> Africans. And Nana, Nana
> carried them with her. Four
> generations of Peazants. And
> we must carry them with us,
> wherever we go.

USE KI-KONGO SYMBOL

                              CUT TO:

[147]

ANGLE ON - NANA PEAZANT AND HAAGAR

They too are watching the photo session. Nana
is curious, Snead is able to capture and
hold "memories" with his camera. Nana relied
on her "scraps of memories" and the "bottle
tree". . .

                    NANA PEAZANT
                 (to Haagar)
            You're a natural fool, Haagar
            Peazant. Nobody ever said that
            the old souls were living
            inside those glass jars. The
            bottle tree reminds us of who
            was here and who's gone on.
            You study on the colors and
            shapes. You appreciate the
            bottle tree each day, as you
            appreciate your loved ones.

BACK TO MR. SNEAD AND VIOLA

Viola is watcing Snead working overtime and
sweating. He is whistling to himself as he
loads another glass negative into is
camera. Amazed by his enthusiasm, Viola is
filled with desire for him. In an unexpected
move, Snead swings Viola around in a circle.

                    VIOLA
                 (shocked)
            Mr. Snead!

                    MR. SNEAD
                 (to Viola)
            Can you take me to the old man,
            Bilal?

                    VIOLA
                 (shaken by Snead's sudden
                  passion)
            That old heathen? He's not
            important.

                    MR. SNEAD
            Is Bilal family?

[148]

                         VIOLA
                  (gathering her wits)
            Oh, I guess so. Everybody back
            off on these islands is family.
            But so many like Bilal are
            so...backward. They believe
            everything is caused by conjure,
            magic or their ancestors. They
            leave nothing to God.

BACK TO HAAGAR AND NANA

Haagar and Nana are still watching Snead and
Viola.

                         HAAGAR
                  (taunting and teasing)
            Where we're heading, Nana,
            there'll be no need for trees
            covered with glass jars in our
            yard. We'll have gardens of
            fresh flowers. Vegetables, for
            the dinner table. Where we're
            heading, Nana, there'll be no
            need for an old woman's magic.

                              DISSOLVE TO:

IN A SERIES OF SHOTS WE SEE:

Mr. Snead taking pictures of the ritual
washing of the feet of the ELDERS by younger
family members.

The family Hairbraider playing with a child's
bubble pipe.

The family is gathered together for a group
portrait. We pull back to reveal a very
animated Mr. Snead scurrying about, shouting,
orchestrating.

                         MR. SNEAD
                  (with passion)
            Look! Look up!... And
            remember...Ibo Landing!

EXT. PICNIC SITE - DAY

Nana, Haagar and Viola are seated on carved
wooden chairs, the other women revolve around
them. Nana is leaning forward as the younger
women wash and groom her feet. The women are
laughing and talking among themselves. Nana
has something in her hands that she is
working on.

ANGLE ON - NANA

Her dark brown face is seen in profile
at intermittent moments against the billowing
white dresses.

CLOSE ON - NANA'S HANDS

Nana is sewing together a small leather pouch,
she's making a "charm bag", better known as a
"Hand".

ON - HAAGAR

Full of vigor, Haagar seems more confident
since her confrontation with Nana. Right now
Haagar is teasing the Newlywed Woman.

                    HAAGAR
                (to Newlywed Woman)
            Can't complain about those
            horseflies bothering
            you. You better stop putting
            that lard on your head.

Viola nervously watches Nana's every move.

                    VIOLA
                (whispering to Nana)
            The Lord will carry us through,
            Nana. Trust in Jesus! Nana, we
            don't need any charms of dried
            roots and flowers...

Nana removes a lock of hair from her tin can.

                    NANA
                (to the women around her)
            When I was child, my mother cut
            this from her hair before she
            was sold away from us.

Nana adds some of her own hair to what she has
saved of her mother's hair. She kisses the
hair and inserts both of them into the "Hand"
that she is creating.

                         NANA (CONT'D)
                Now, I'm adding my own hair.
                There must be a bond ...a
                connection, between those that
                go up North, and those who across
                the sea. A connection!
                         (a few beats, then)
                We are as two people in one body.
                The last of the old, and the
                first of the new. We will always
                live this double life, you know,
                because we're from the sea. We
                came here in chains, and we must
                survive. We must survive.
                There's salt-water in our
                blood. . .

EXT. PICNIC SITE - MEN'S GROUP - DAY

We hear Bilal O.S. speaking in French to Mr.
Snead. Nearby, other men are crouching,
figuring out roads and trails in the dusty
ground, they turn their attention to
Bilal and Mr. Snead.

                         BILAL
                         (to Snead, in French)
                [They bring me here, as a boy,
                 from the colonies in the French
                 West Indies.]

                         MR. SNEAD
                         (to Bilal, in French)
                [When...? What do you remember?
                 Do you remember your home. Your
                 family?]

                         BILAL
                         (to Snead, in English)
                Mister, for many years I have
                not spoken these words. What
                I remember I'll tell you in the
                language I learned to speak here.
                I came here on a ship called "The
                Wanderer." I came with the Ibo.

                         (more)

[151]

                              BILAL (CONT'D)
                         (recollecting the tragedy)
                    Some say the Ibo flew back home
                    to Africa. Some say they all
                    joined hands and walked on top
                    of the water. But, Mister, I was
                    there. Those Ibo, men, women
                    and children, a hundred or more,
                    shackled in iron...when they
                    went down in that water, they
                    never came up. Ain't nobody can
                    walk on water.

          CLOSE ON - ELI

          Listening to Bilal's words, coming to grips
          with his own transformation.

          BACK TO WOMEN - PICNIC SITE

          Trula watches Yellow Mary with her family;
          in the last few hours, a curious distance
          has developed between them.

          The women continue to fuss over Nana as she
          sews the "Hand." Nana is constructing the
          "Hand" to protect her family, at a feverish
          pitch.

                              HAAGAR
                         (curtly)
                    We'll be fine, Nana.

                              VIOLA
                         (deeply concerned)
                    Now, Nana, don't you go
                    worrying. We're going to be
                    just fine.

          Nana ignores them, adding bits and pieces of
          the "scraps of memories" from her tin can
          into the "Hand".

          Viola is weeping for Nana; the creation of the
          "Hand" frightens her.

                              HAAGAR
                         (taking control)
                    'Mind now, Nana Peazant. Don't
                    go work yourself up. It's too
                    hot out here for no mess.
                         (sharply to Viola)
                    Get a hold of yourself, Viola!

BACK TO MEN'S GROUP

Daddy Mac is talking to Mr. Snead and the
other men.

> DADDY MAC
> (to Mr. Snead)
> I remember what my father taught
> me before he passed on. It was
> the same as his father taught
> him on the day he became a man.
> He said, "Women are the sweetness
> of life," Mr. Snead. "They're
> sweet to the eye, cause they're
> beautiful. They're sweet to the
> ears, because of their lovely
> voice, and the way they sing.
> Women are the sweetness of life,"
> and that's what I remember.

The men react to the sound of Nana Peazant
sobbing loudly.

BACK TO WOMEN'S GROUP

Nana throws back her head and unleashes a
woefull field cry. She sobs aloud, like
she did as a child, alone in the world with
only a lock of her mother's hair to comfort
and protect her.

Nana rises to run away. She is stopped by
Yellow Mary, as the family gathers around.

> YELLOW MARY
> (to Nana, cutting in, trying
> to calm her)
> I've been on my own since I was
> a little girl.
> (struggling to find the
> right words)
> I've been on my own for such a
> long time, I thought I wanted it
> to be that way...

> HAAGAR
> (out loud to everyone,
> looking for a laugh)
> Lord knows, you've worked hard,
> gal.

                        YELLOW MARY
                     (to Nana)
            You know I'm not like the other
            women here. But I need to know
            that I can come home,... to hold
            on to what I come from. I need
            to know that the people here know
            my name.
                     (shouting, for everyone to
                      hear)
            I'm Yellow Mary Peazant! And
            I'm a proud woman, not a hard
            woman.
                     (softly, to Nana)
            I want to stay. I want to stay
            and visit with you here.

                        HAAGAR
                     (shocked)
            What!!!
                     (about Yellow Mary)
            Now how's she going to come and
            put her shame on Mother Peazant?

ANGLE ON - OTHER PEAZANT WOMEN

CAMERA pans across them arguing.

                        NANA PEAZANT
                     (weeping)
            I can't understand how me and
            Peazant put you children here
            on earth to fight among
            yourselves. How you can leave
            this soil... this soil. The
            sweat of our love, it's here
            in this soil. I love you 'cause
            you're mine.
                     (sobbing)
            You're the fruit of an ancient
            tree.

ANGLE ON - EULA

She springs forth to defend Yellow Mary. Eula
loses her balance.

                        EULA
            Hush! Hush! Hush, all of you.

Eula is sickened by their talk. She directs
her anger, not only to Haagar, but to the
other women who eagerly joined in the attack
on Yellow Mary.

[154]

                    EULA
                (continues)
            Some of us aren't forgetting how
            Yellow Mary sent the money to get
            Cousin Jake out of jail last
            spring...

ANGLE ON - HAAGAR

Interrupting,

                    HAAGAR
            Now, Nana, we aren't talking
            about no Cousin Jake here.
                (to Yellow Mary)
            A dog don't get mad 'cause you
            say he's a dog!

ANGLE ON - ELI

Cutting in,

                    ELI
                (shouting to Eula)
            Say it!

ANGLE ON - EULA

Her anger, quick movements, and advanced state
of pregnancy are causing her noticeable
distress. Eula fights to hold back the bitter
bile rising in her throat.

                    EULA
            If you're so ashamed of Yellow
            Mary 'cause she got ruined. . .
            Well, what do you say about
            me?
                (gesturing to her pregnant
                stomach)
            Am I ruined, too?

The women freeze in mid-motion, their mouths
open, gaping. Sexual abuse, a legacy of
slavery, is a part of their unspoken history.
Hearing Eula's words, the women are "shamed"
for Eli and respectfully turn their faces away
from him.

ANGLE ON - ELI

                        ELI
                  (softly, to Eula)
            Whatever's to be said, just say
            it now, Eula!

                        EULA
                  (in a rush of emotions)
            As far as this placed is concerned,
            we never enjoyed our womanhood...
            Deep inside, we believed that
            they ruined our mothers, and
            their mothers before them. And
            we live our lives always expecting
            the worst because we feel we
            don't deserve any better.
                  (a few beats, then)
            Deep inside we believe that even
            God can't heal the wounds of our
            past or protect us from the world
            that put shackles on our feet.

CLOSE ON - VIOLA

She winces in recognition, but attempts to
cover her feelings. She hides within the
cloak of her religion.

                        VIOLA
                  (cutting in for Jesus)
            My God loves me and protects me
            and watches over me.

                        EULA
                  (to the women)
            Even though you're going up
            North, you all think about being
            ruined, too. You think you can
            cross over to the mainland and
            run away from it? You're going
            to be sorry, sorry if you don't
            change your way of thinking
            before you leave this place.

Eula, turning away from the group, vomits onto
the ground. One woman tries to help her but
Eula waves her away, and with her back to her
family she continues.

                    EULA (CONT'D)
                 (continues)
        If you love yourselves, then
        love Yellow Mary, because she's
        a part of you. Just like we're
        a part of our mothers. A lot
        of us are going through things
        we feel we can't handle all
        alone.

ANGLE ON - IONA, MYOWN, YELLOW MARY, NANA
PEAZANT

                    EULA
                 (to Iona, and the younger
                  woman)
        There's going to be all kinds of
        roads to take in life... Let's
        not be afraid to take them. We
        deserve them, because we're all
        good women.

Hugging an older woman,

                    EULA
        Do you... do you understand...
        who we are, and what we have
        become?

She picks up Nana's tin can.

                    EULA
        We're the daughters of those old
        dusty things Nana carries in
        her tin can...
                 (pausing)
        We carry too many scars from the
        past. Our past owns us. We
        wear our scars like armor,
        ...for protection. Our mother's
        scars, our sister's scars, our
        daughter's scars... Thick,
        hard, ugly scars that no one can
        pass through to ever hurt us
        again. Let's live our lives
        without living in the fold of
        old wounds.

Nana, Yellow Mary and Eula embrace.

                    CUT TO:

[157]

FLASHBACK - EXT. SHAD PEAZANT'S FIELD - DAY

ANGLE ON - YOUNG NANA PEAZANT

As a YOUNG WOMAN, NANA PEAZANT is running
forward. She makes her way up a dusty road
approaching a young man planting seeds in
the earth. The way he is planting is very
different, it's an ancient African method,
using the heel and toe of the same foot. The
man is SHAD PEAZANT, her husband.

CLOSE ON - YOUNG NANA PEAZANT

She squats down with her arms outstretched
until her husband, Shad, reaches her at the
edge of the field.

ON - YOUNG NANA'S HANDS

The soil, like dust, blows from her hands and
through her fingers.

                    YOUNG NANA PEAZANT
                 (to her husband)
            Shad, how can we plant in this
            dust?

                    SHAD
                 (to Nana)
            We plant each and every year, or
            we're finished!

END FLASHBACK

                                 CUT TO:

EXT. IBO LANDING - DAY

The family gathers at Ibo Landing. Nana leads
them through a religious ceremony, "A Root
Revival of Love."

                    NANA PEAZANT
                 (solemnly)
            My life is almost over, and yours
            is just starting. And I'm not
            going to live long enough to see
            what becomes of all you "free
            Negroes."

ANGLE ON - VIOLA

She is exhausted from weeping.

>   VIOLA
>   (cutting in, for Jesus)
>   We're going to be watching from
>   heaven, Nana.

ANGLE ON - NANA PEAZANT

>   NANA PEAZANT
>   No! I'm not going to be watching
>   from heaven while there's soil
>   still here for me for planting.

ANGLE ON - CHARM BAG

Nana Peazant holds up the "Hand" she has made,
the St. Christopher's charm is wrapped around
it. She takes Viola's Bible and lays the
"Hand" on top of it. Then, with a firm
grip, Nana takes a hold of Bilal's shoulder.

>   NANA PEAZANT
>   (holding up her "Hand")
>   We've taken old Gods and given
>   them new names. They saw it all
>   here that day, those Ibo.

She holds her "Hand," on top of Viola's Bible,
out to her family. We HEAR the SOUND of other
Black families in the region giving voice to
FIELD CRIES. Cries that fall upon the Peazant
Family gathering as a blessing.

>   NANA PEAZANT
>   (indicating contents of her
>   "Hand")
>   This "Hand," it's from me, from
>   us, from them (the Ibo)... Just
>   like all of you... Come
>   children, kiss this hand full of
>   me.

ANGLE ON - VIOLA

Who is set off again by Nana's root working.

>   VIOLA
>   (frightened by Nana's words)
>   Lord, have mercy, have mercy.

ANGLE ON - NANA PEAZANT

And like those old Ibos, Nana Peazant calls
upon the womb of time to help shatter the
temporal restrictions of her own existence -
to become a being who is beyond death, beyond
aging, beyond time.

                    NANA PEAZANT
              (holding up her "Hand" and
               Bible)
              Take my "Hand."   I'm the one that
          can give you strength.

The family comes forward to kiss the "Hand."

ANGLE ON - ELI, EULA, AND YELLOW MARY

They fall to their knees before Nana Peazant.

ANGLE ON - NANA PEAZANT

                    NANA PEAZANT
                 (continuing)
              Take me wherever you go. I'm
              your strength.

ANGLE ON - TRULA

Who has been watchng the ritual from a
distance. Trula does not understand what
is happening, but she realizes that Yellow
Mary will not be leaving with her the next
morning. Trula runs away from the ceremony.

ANGLE ON - PEAZANT FAMILY

The family takes communion from their
great-grandmother, immersing themselves in
their traditions ons and culture. Suddenly
Viola begins the scream.

ANGLE ON - VIOLA

Viola wants her shot at heaven, she is out of
control and screaming.

ANGLE ON - VIOLA

                         VIOLA
                  (shouting to Nana)
            Old folks supposed to die!
                     (weeping)
            It's not right! We're supposed
            to die and go to heaven! What
            you're doing is wrong...

ANOTHER ANGLE

As more and more women and men join in the
ritual of spirit regeneration, Viola and
Haagar try to hold them back from Nana
Peazant.

ANGLE ON - HAAGAR

With self-righteous indignation, she is moved
to physical anger. Haagar strikes out at her
daughters, Myown and Iona, who want to be a
part of Nana's spirit regeneration ceremony.
Other family members have to pull Haagar off
of her daughters.

                        HAAGAR
            Hoodoo..Hoodoo! Hoodoo mess!
            Ain't no roots and herbs going
            to change nothing. Don't go and
            spoil everything! Old
            Used-To-Do-It-This-Way don't help
            none today!

Haagar walks away, she looks back in anger,
ignoring Nana's open arms and the pleas from
her own daughters. Haagar turns inward,
perhaps to remain unenlightened and
disenfranchised forever.

WIDE ANGLE ON FAMILY

                    NANA PEAZANT
                (pleading with Haagar)
            Come, come child... I love you
            'cause you're mine!

                        MYOWN
                (crying out to Haagar)
            Mama, please!

[161]

ANGLE ON VIOLA

Viola watches Mr. Snead join her family in
fellowship. Snead approaches Viola with
caution, then he grabs a hold of Viola,
lifting her off the ground as he kisses her.

ANGLE ON - NANA PEAZANT

We can see the sorrow in her face, she has
lost Haagar. She looks over to her family,
they are hugging and kissing one another.
They are her future.

ANGLE ON - VIOLA, NANA, AND MR. SNEAD

Viola kisses her Bible, and then pecks a
smaller kiss on a section of Nana Peazant's
"Hand."

                                    FADE TO:

EXT. IBO LANDING - DAY

Bilal Muhammed is performing his morning
prayers, just as he always has and always
will on this island by the sea. His crudely
written Arabic words are fading within the
pages of his homemade Koran.

                                 DISSOLVE TO:

EXT. BEACH - DAY

St. Julian Last Child, on horseback, is
galloping along a deserted beach. The last
child born of the Cherokee Nation to inhabit
this island.

                                    CUT TO:

EXT. IBO LANDING - DAY

On the marshy banks of Ibo Landing. The
family is at the dock, loading the boat and
getting ready to depart. Iona is anxiously
pacing, we assume that she is looking for
Myown, who comes running up late. Nana stands
apart, watching their preparations.

                    NANA PEAZANT (O.S.)
                      (narrating)
            In this quiet place, simple folk
            knelt down and caught a glimpse
            of the eternal.

Family members wave to Nana.

                    NANA PEAZANT
            Morning would begin a new life
            for my children and me. They
            would carry my spirit. I would
            remain here, with the old souls.

ANGLE ON - ST. JULIAN LAST CHILD

On horseback, galloping up to the barge.

ANGLE ON IONA

She jumps from the barge and runs towards him.
Haagar calls out to Iona, but she is
restrained by her family. Iona mounts St.
Julien Last Child's horse in a single leap.

                    HAAGAR
                      (screaming)
            Iona! Iona! I...Own...Her!

Iona and her Native American lover gallop
past Nana into yet another destiny.

Haagar sobs uncontrollably.

                              CUT TO:

EXT. IBO LANDING - DAY

The family begin their journey up the river.
They are leaving their personal history and
entering upon the larger history of the
African diaspora.

ON - MYOWN

Her eyes are filled with tears and with
wonder. She's wearing Nana's "Hand" around her
neck, she carries Yellow Mary's
"store-brought" Uneeda Biscuit tin can.

Haagar holds onto Ninnyjugs and weeps. She
has realized her long-awaited passage from
Ibo Landing. Haagar's transit fee, paid to
the old souls, is the leaving behind of her
daughter, Iona.

> UNBORN CHILD (O.S)
> (recollecting)
> And so, on the 19th day of August,
> 1902, they left these islands,
> having said farewell, perhaps
> never to see us again.

> CUT TO:

EXT. BEACH - DAY

ON - NANA PEAZANT, EULA, AND YELLOW MARY

Walking across the horizon.

> UNBORN CHILD (O.S.)
> (recollecting)
> My Momma and Daddy stayed behind
> with Yellow Mary. Some say Eli
> got himself all involved with
> the anti-lynching issue. Some
> say Eula saw too much of herself
> in Nana Peazant, and wanted her
> children born on this island.
> They say Mama was always
> peculiar and Nana's roots and
> herbs set her off. All I know
> is, I was born here before Nana
> passed on.

The Unborn Child is running behind them in
SLOW MOTION. And while they are walking,
each woman individually turns to dust and
blows into the burning sun.

> UNBORN CHILD (V.O.)
> (recollecting)
> We remained behind, growing
> older, wiser, stronger.

The Unborn Child remains alone, along the
horizon.

FADE OUT.

Gullah Translation

UBC NARRATION - GULLAH DIALECT

A am de firs an de las. A am de honored one an de scorn. A am
de whore an de holy one. A am the wife an de virgin. A am de
barren one and many are my dahtas. A am de silence that you
cannot understan. A am de utterance of my name.

My story begin on de eve of my family migration Nort. My story
begin. . .befo A was born.

Nana pray for help...I got dere jus en time...

My great great grandmudda, Nana Peazant, saw de family comin'
apart. Her flowers ta bloom en a distan frontier. An then,
dere was my Ma an Daddy's problem...

Nana pray an de ol' souls guided me ento de New Worl. A come en
time for de big celebration, ta be among my cousins, my aunties
an uncles... A cayn still see their faces, smell de oil en de
wicker lamp... A cayn year the voice of Auntie Haagar callin
out for her dauhtas Iona and Myown, and teasin de newlyweds. . .

It was an age of beginings, a time of promises. . . The
newspaper say it was a time for everyone, the rich an de poor,
de powerful an the powerless.

My time was running out. The oomen were arguin' and fightin'
amongst themselves. A can still see de fear an de hope in de
eyes of our fathers. De sons of drums. . .who could only speak
of their future. Everyone was jus as scared as Nana Peazant.

A was travelin' on a spritual mission, but sometimes A would get
distracted....

There was a time when the colored woman was beaten back into
slavery by fear. . . My Ma's fears overwhelm me. . .

A remember how important de children were to the Peazant family
an how A had to convince my Daddy that I was his child. Years
later, my Ma told me she knew that A had been sent forward by de
ol' souls. . . My, Ma said she could feel me by her side.

A remember de call of my grea grea grandmudda. . . A remember
de journey home... A remember de long walk ta de family
graveyard, ta de house that A would be born in, . . . ta de
picnic site. A remember an A recall.

It take great strength to let go of somethin' that you have
created, but the seperation is often necessary for somethin' new
to emerge.

We left our markers in the soil, ...in memory of the families
who onced lived here... We were the children of those who chose
to survive.

En dis quiet place, year ago, my family knelt down an caught a
glimpse of de eternal. . .

En dis quiet place, year ago, we knelt down an caught a glimpse
of de eternal. . .

And so, on the 19th day of Augus, 1902, dey left these islants
an set out for de Nort havin' said farewell, perhaps never to
see us again..

My Ma and Daddy stay behin' wit Yella Mary. Some say Eli got
himself all involved wit de anti-lynchin issue. Some say Eula
saw too much of herself in Nana Peazant, wanted her children
born on dis islan. Dey say Ma was always peculiar an Nana's
roots an herbs set she off. . .   All A know is that A was bawn
here befor Nana pass on. . .   An, we remain behin' growin'
older, wiser, stronger.

Filmography

Daughters Of The Dust,
35MM FEATURE FILM, 1992

Lost In The Night,
35MM MUSIC VIDEO, 1992

Praise House,
16MM SHORT, MADE FOR TELEVISION, 1991

Relatives,
SUPER-8 SHORT, MADE FOR TELEVISION, 1990

Phyliss Wheatly, YWCA,
INDUSTRIAL SHORT 1989

Preventing Cancer,
INDUSTRIAL SHORT, MOREHOUSE SCHOOL OF MEDICINE 1989

Breaking The Silence,
VIDEO, NATIONAL BLACK WOMEN'S HEALTH PROJECT, 1988

Illusions,
16MM SHORT 1983

Four Women,
16MM SHORT 1975

Diary Of An African Nun,
16MM SHORT 1977

Working Models Of Success,
16MM DOCUMENTARY 1973

Awards for *Daughters of the Dust* and Julie Dash

1990

Black Filmakers Hall of Fame
New Voices, New Vision

1991

Sundance Film Festival
Best Cinematography

CEBA Award
Pioneer of Excellence

Vesta Award
Media & Visual Arts

Black Filmakers Hall of Fame
Oscar Micheaux Award

National Black Programming Consortium
Prized Pieces—Best Independent Producer

National Black Programming Consortium
Prized Pieces—Best Drama

1992

Black Oscar
Special Recognition Award

Black Filmakers Hall of Fame
Best Film

Coalition of 100 Black Women
Candence Award, Trailblazer

Women in Film
Special Merit Certificate, Crystal Award

American Film Institute
Maya Deren Award

*Certificate of appreciation, "First feature length film
in theatrical distribution by an African American woman."*
Maxine Waters, Member of Congress,
29th District (3/3/92)

Daughters of the Dust

SELECTED READING LIST

Carawan, Guy and Candie, *Ain't You Got a Right to the Tree of Life?: The People of Johns Island, South Carolina—Their Faces, Their Words, and Their Songs*, (University of Georgia Press, Athens, [GA], 1989).

Creel, Margaret Washington, *A Peculiar People: Slave Religion and Community-Culture Among the Gullahs*, (New York University Press, New York, 1988).

Daise, Ronald, *Reminiscences of Sea Island Heritage*, (Sandlapper Pub., Orangeburg, [SC], 1987).

Georgia Writers' Project, Savannah Unit, *Drums and Shadows: Survival Studies Among the Georgia Coastal Negroes*, (University of Georgia Press, Athens, [GA], 1986).

Herskovits, Melville J., *The Myth of the Negro Past*, (Beacon Press, Boston, 1990).

Jones-Jackson, Patricia, *When Roots Die: Endangered Traditions on the Sea Islands*, (University of Georgia Press, Athens, [GA], 1986).

Moutoussamy-Ashe, Jeanne, *Daufuskie Island, a Photographic Essay*, (University of South Carolina Press, Columbus, [SC], 1982).

Thompson, Robert Farris, *Flash of the Spirit: African and Afro-American Art and Philosophy*, (Random House, New York, 1983).

—and Joseph Cornet, *The Four Moments of the Sun: Kongo Art in Two Worlds*, (National Gallery of Art, Washington, D.C., 1981).